Lighthouse Ghosts and Legends

Cover photograph
of Cape Neddick Nubble
Light by John Murray

Every effort has been made to trace copyright holders. Crane Hill Publishers
apologizes for any unintentional omissions and would be pleased, in such cases,
to add an acknowledgment in future editions.

Published by Crane Hill Publishers, www.cranehill.com

Printed in the United States of America

Library of Congress Cataloging-in-Publication Data

Costopoulos, Nina.
  Lighthhouse ghosts and legends / by Nina Costopoulos.
     p. cm.
Includes bibliographical references.
  ISBN 1-57587-173-4
 1. Haunted places--United States. 2. Ghosts--United States. 3.
Legends--United States. 4. Lighthouses--Folklore. I. Title.
  BF1472.U6 C67 2003
   133.1'22--dc21
                              2002153679

10   9   8   7   6   5   4   3   2   1

Lighthouse Ghosts and Legends

Nina Costopoulos

CRANE HILL
PUBLISHERS

Contents

Introduction

As lighthouse enthusiasts will attest, there's just
something about lighthouses that fascinates us—
something more than the proud legacy for which they
stand, something more than their example of man's
ingenuity, or their reminder of nature's indifference,
something that captures the imagination.

In early American coastal life, some degree of fas-
cination with lighthouses was necessary. After all,
families depended on sea trade; whole communities
revolved around it. Husbands, sons, and brothers
took to the sea, becoming sailors or fishermen. And
the generations who came to rely on the mercy of the
deep prayed for a light in the storm. Over the years,
this prayer grew into a crusade to shine a light on our
nation's coasts. One by one, lights like Hendricks
Head, Neddick Nubble, and Carysfort Reef sprang up
as if in answer to a clarion call. These lights, and
others like them up and down the Atlantic and Pacific
coasts, truly were saviors—to the ships that passed in
the night, to the wives and children of the seamen
aboard those ships, and to the merchants expecting
a swift and safe delivery of their goods. The lights
shouldered the burden of coastal life, and, in so
doing, became larger than life. To the early-American
families who lived and died by the tide, lighthouses
represented hope and perseverance. All eyes were
on them.

Ironically, lighthouse keepers, often altogether cut
off from society, were, quite literally, at the center of
this societal preoccupation. As a matter of course,

people who were anxious about their duties became curious about their lives—not only where they lived, but how they lived. Of course, public interest didn't often translate into public empathy. Much has been made of the profound loneliness suffered by lighthouse keepers and their families. And many tales have been told of these desperate individuals going mad from isolation and taking their own, or others', lives. They were constant fixtures in the consciousness of their communities, but this was likely of little consolation to them on cold and desolate nights, when the light and the task of tending it were their only companions.

Yet, clearly, lighthouse keepers had some sense of their consequence and the consequence of their charge. After all, on an almost daily basis, they risked life and limb in the name of duty. Tales abound of their courage, their loyalty, and their humanity. Even when their names have been forgotten, their stories have not. In this way, they've remained, as they always were, a subject of profound curiosity, woven forever into the fabric of legend and local lore.

Today, much has changed. We no longer rely on lighthouses to the degree we once did. A sailor's life no longer revolves around the dangers of the deep and the mercy of Mother Nature. Ship's captains chart their courses with computers, according to satellite-generated weather forecasts; and technological advances like sonar and radar have made the warning lights of many a tower more or less obsolete.

Two hundred years ago, lighthouses were popping up all along America's coasts. These days, the trend is reversed—the lights are going out. But, though many a powerful beam has been darkened, the power of lighthouses over us has not been dimmed. We are fascinated still by these strong sentinels, the tragedies and triumphs they must have seen. Undoubtedly, after more than two hundred years, they have stories yet to tell. And there are stories still to be told of them, as well as mysteries to be solved.

In the end, with all of their intrigue, there is little wonder that lighthouses fascinate us. All we have to do is consider their great service to our country, and the unending devotion they inspired in those who served them. Perhaps, because they were at the center of coastal life for so many years, there is an energy that surrounds them still, some sort of centripetal force that draws the eye and then the imagination. It's as if, somewhere in our subconscious, we sense the steady pulse of their beacons calling us into port. And so, apparently, do the wandering and restless spirits whose tales fill the pages of this book. Like ships lost at sea, they also are drawn into the light.

Georgetown Light
North Island, South Carolina

Warning on Winyah Bay

Georgetown Light
North Island, South Carolina

Ravaged by brutal storms that sweep across the Atlantic, coastal South Carolina has seen vast destruction and loss. It is a capricious and often cruel environment, where, for several hundred years, lighthouses have proved crucial to the survival of seafarers. South Carolina's oldest active lighthouse, the Georgetown Light, sits at the mouth of Winyah Bay, 12 miles from Georgetown, South Carolina, on North Island. To locals, it is known as the North Island Light.

North Island's first lighthouse was built of cypress wood in 1801. Six years later, it was toppled by a massive storm. Wary of wood's ability to withstand violent weather, the new contractors chose to construct an 87-foot brick tower in 1812. Over the years, the tower survived a number of trials, such as South Carolina's legendary hurricanes. In 1857, it was equipped with a fourth-order Fresnel lense. Despite the contractors good intentions, the lighthouse was damaged during the Civil War. Then, in 1867, builders reconstructed a lighthouse with stone walls as thick as 6 feet at the base, and the waves that lashed the coastline had met their match. Even the tower's spiral staircase, with its 124 steps, was cut from stone rather than the cast iron common to other lighthouses. The stone lighthouse still stands today.

The Georgetown Light survived a succession of keepers over the years as well, and many a story has been told of their lives. But one story above all is remembered on North Island. In the early 1800s, a new keeper arrived at the lighthouse with his young daughter, Annie. The fair-haired child was small, and her father was protective. As Annie was too young to care for herself, the pair went everywhere together. She shadowed her father as he kept the large whale-oil lantern burning, and when they ran low on food and supplies, father and daughter climbed aboard their tiny rowboat and set off for Georgetown.

Annie's father, like many keepers of his day, had taken on the added responsibility of serving also as a weatherman during his tenure at the light. However, with little more than rudimentary instruments, weather patterns were difficult to predict—especially in the bay. His forecasts were often accurate, but the danger of an unforeseen storm always loomed.

Such was the case one sunny day. The keeper and his daughter set off to the mainland to replenish supplies. With no sign of inclement weather—the water was calm, the sun warm, and the breeze soft—the happy companions decided to take advantage of the pleasant day. They shopped leisurely, leaving just enough time to row back before dark. As the day wore on, a warm but brisk wind rolled across the water and through town. Always cautious, the keeper scrutinized the sky to see if the weather was turning. Sure enough, though he found the sky still blue, gray storm clouds were crowding the horizon. Fearful of getting caught in a storm, the two filled their small craft with supplies and started rowing home.

In no time, heavy, stinging raindrops and hail began to fall across the water. The keeper used all of his strength to row, but the winds grew fierce, and the waters kicked up violent, savage waves. Soon, rain began to fill the small boat. Young Annie sat huddled and shivering as her father fought helplessly against the swelling waves.

The two had completed three-quarters of their trip when waves spilled over the sides of the boat, nearly flooding it. The keeper knew they were going to sink. In desperation, he gathered Annie up and tied her to his back. Already weary, he had no choice but to swim the rest of the way to shore. Annie held tight, but as her father fought the impossible current, the waters engulfed her time and again. Almost drowned, the keeper pushed forward until, at last, he crawled to shore and collapsed. When he awoke hours later, he found his beloved daughter still strapped to his back, lifeless. He had lost her to the sea.

For many months, the keeper mourned the tragic death of his daughter, Annie. He found it hard to man the lighthouse; there were constant reminders of her companionship in all he did. Often, when he went inland, locals noticed him wandering the streets, despondent and confused. He walked through town, weary and saddened, calling out for Annie as though she were simply playing a game of hide-and-seek.

Those who have heard the tale believe that the heartbroken keeper never truly recovered from the death of his dear Annie. He simply found his duty too much to bear. Annie, however, is as dedicated as ever. Local legend claims that Annie's ghost has remained on and about North Island to warn sailors of sudden changes in the weather. Ever since her death, seafarers have reported seeing a sweet blonde child who mysteriously appears aboard their vessel. Often, she appears during warm, sunny weather—like the weather she experienced on her last trip into town—and warns sailors to return to the mainland.

Many have been startled enough by the specter of the fair-haired child to heed her warning and seek solid ground. Others, who have ignored her warning, have met her dreadful fate. For, sure enough, despite all indications to the contrary, shortly after she appears, the weather turns abruptly violent, slamming mammoth waves into the coast and sealing the doom of anyone still afloat.

Today, the keeper's dwelling no longer stands. The lighthouse, however, is an active navigational aid listed on the National Historic Register. As the island is now privately owned, the lighthouse is closed to the public, though the owners do allow visitors to walk up the beach to the high-tide mark. The island is accessible only by boat. Tours are available through Low Country Plantation Tours, 843-477-0287. Website: lowcountrytours.com

Cape Neddick Nubble Light
York Beach, Maine

A Light Too Late in Coming

Cape Neddick Nubble Light
York Beach, Maine

The legend of the ghost ship Isadore has been told and retold for more than a century along the blustery coast of Maine, where the rocky, treacherous cliffs of island Cape Neddick Nubble have sealed the doom of many a sailor. Here, jagged outcroppings known as the Bald Head Cliffs stretch northward into the icy waters, creating perilous conditions.

In 1837, Captain Joseph Smith petitioned for lighthouses on York River and Cape Neddick Nubble. Moneys were allocated for a small lighthouse at York Ledge, but the cape remained dark, and schooners continued to be lost against the treacherous Bald Head Cliffs. When another petition was introduced in 1852, Congress allocated $5,000 for a beacon; but after an inspection of the area, the project floundered. Then, in 1874, Congress appropriated $15,000 for a lighthouse. On July 1, 1879, the Cape Neddick Nubble beacon was finally lit 88 feet above the water.

Unfortunately, the light had come too late for

many a fearless seafarer, particularly thirty-six-year-old Captain Leander Foss and his crew aboard the *Isadore*. The ship set sail November 30, 1842, from Kennebunkport harbor, despite the strong misgivings of its crew.

Two nights before the *Isadore's* departure, Thomas King, a young seaman who had received a month's wages in advance for his anticipated tenure, had a nightmare. He dreamt of turbulent waters, the ship wrecked amid a swirling storm, and all aboard doomed. Shaken, King relayed his premonition to Captain Foss, whose scorn turned to suspicion when King requested to be relieved of his duties. Unwilling to give up the young seaman or the wages already paid to him, the captain would not let King out of his contract. Dispirited, King weighed his options but couldn't reconcile himself to the journey. In the end, whatever the consequences, he refused the captain's order. Instead of boarding the ship with the other crewmembers, King hid in the nearby woods. An angry Captain Foss ordered the crew to search the port and surrounding areas for King. Despite a burgeoning snowstorm that threatened their departure, the men searched relentlessly until evening but found no trace of their missing crewman. Finally, on that fateful Thanksgiving night, the *Isadore* set sail without Thomas King.

Unbeknownst to King, another crewman had dreamt of the ship's demise as well. In his dream the crewman had seen seven coffins, including his own, washed up on Maine's shoreline. Like King, he had told others of his dream, but no one had taken his apprehension to heart. He set sail along with the others.

Nineteen-year-old William Thomson was also aboard the *Isadore* that day. It was to be his first journey at sea, and he was filled with nervous excitement. His mother, who adamantly opposed the life that her husband had urged their son into, was filled with a nameless dread. She had wanted William to be a farmer, safe and sound on dry land.

Aside even from the warnings and premonitions of Thomas King, there was something ominous about the ship's departure that November day. The snowstorm had ushered in violent winds, and visibility was poor. Crew members and their families, who had gathered along the wharf to see them off, were equally concerned that the day was unfit for sailing. It was later rumored that, even as the ship drifted out to sea, the men onboard could hear the wails of their wives and mothers out on the wharf.

Those watching and weeping on the wharf were eventually blinded by the snow, and the ship was lost from sight. Not long after, the dreaded news arrived from Ogunquit: the *Isadore* had wrecked in the Bald Head Cliffs north of Cape Neddick Nubble. Already, the lifeless bodies and splintery remains of the ship had begun to wash ashore. All were lost: Captain Leander Foss, the young crewman who had dreamt of the seven coffins, and William Thomson. The sole survivor was Thomas King, who narrowly escaped death in the snowy woods of Kennebunkport harbor.

Ever since the *Isadore* was lost in the jagged rocks of Bald Head Cliffs, locals, particularly fishermen and those standing watch at the Cape Neddick Nubble Light, have reported seeing the shadowy likeness of a ship sailing up and down the coast. One fisherman claimed to see men on board the ship. They stared straight ahead as they passed from view, diligently working their stations though their clothes dripped with water.

The *Isadore* and its crew are still believed to haunt the waters off the northern coast of Maine. Most often, sightings occur where the Cape Neddick Nubble Light now stands. If only it had been standing that November night so many years ago.

From U.S. 1 in York, take Route 1A. At York Beach, turn right on Nubble Road. Follow Nubble Road to Nubble Point near Long Sands Beach. Though the lighthouse and grounds are not open to the public, parking is free at Sohier Park, which offers an excellent view. For further information, contact Friends of Nubble Light: 186 York Street, York, Maine 03909.

Lighthouse cruises are available through Finestkind Scenic Cruises. Cruises are available May 1 through mid-October. The Nubble Lighthouse Cruise offers a leisurely ride with scenic views of York's elegant homes and rocky coastline. At fourteen miles round-trip, it is Finestkind's longest cruise. For more information, contact Finestkind Scenic Cruises: P.O. Box 1828, Ogunquit, Maine 03907, 207-646-5227; fax: 207-646-4513; email: info@finestkindcruises.com

Bryan Penberthy

Ocracoke Light
Ocracoke Island, North Carolina

Here Walks the Ghost of William Teach

Ocracoke Light
Ocracoke Island, North Carolina

Ocracoke Island was discovered in 1585 when a group of English explorers wrecked its ship into the island's sandy shores. However, it remained undeveloped for roughly two centuries. Today, Ocracoke is one of the North Carolina coast's oldest communities; and with only about 800 year-round residents, it maintains a markedly slower pace than the mainland. Sometimes, when lightning knocks out power on the island, residents rely on the Ocracoke Light to get them through the night, just as they used to do in the old days. Such occasions afford the perfect opportunity to gather around a fire and tell blood-curdling tales of the island's past.

The first lighthouse in the Ocracoke inlet was built on Shell Castle Island in 1794; but due to a migration of the channel, it was useless by 1818—the year it was struck and destroyed by lightning. By 1822, the government had appropriated $20,000 for a new structure on Ocracoke Island. It was build by Noah Porter for $11,359.35. Today, at 179 years of age, it is the second-oldest working lighthouse in the country. It is also, at 75 feet, the shortest lighthouse on the North Carolina coast.

The waters off the North Carolina coast have sunk more than 2,000 ships since authorities started keeping records in 1526. Here, in the outer banks, ships hug the coastline to avoid the havoc of the warm Gulf Stream and icy Labrador Current. Add to that the area's ever-changing sandbars and dangerous Diamond Shoals, and the coast is ripe for maritime disaster. Not surprisingly, it's come to be known as the "Graveyard of the Atlantic." With a name like that, it's bound to host a number of local legends—not the least of which concerns the country's most famous brigand, Edward Teach, otherwise known as Blackbeard, the pirate.

Over the years, many versions of Blackbeard's story have evolved. One version even goes so far as to suggest that he is responsible for Ocracoke's unusual name. According to legend, on the morning of his death, before dawn, the pirate tossed and turned, impatient for daylight. Finally, at his wit's end, he cried, "Oh, cock, crow!" thus giving the island its name. While the tale is likely a tall one, this is certain: Blackbeard called Ocracoke home and met with a grisly death on its shores.

During the 1700s, Ocracoke was one of the busiest inlets on the East Coast. At that time, it was the only accessible waterway to Carolina port cities like

Edmonton and New Bern. Eventually, it got a reputation. With the large number of vessels carrying goods to be sold, crime was inevitable. Pirates attacked and robbed ships, and kidnapped and even murdered sailors. The most infamous marauder of them all was a wealthy Englishman, Edward Teach, whose name came to be known and feared in the outer banks.

A restless spirit drove Teach from a privileged life. Bored with tradition, he turned to a life at sea, pillaging unsuspecting ships for sport. Though he wanted for little as an aristocrat, he made an unprecedented fortune pirating, and he built grand homes with dirty money in Bath, North Carolina, and on Ocracoke Island. He is even said to have had thirteen wives.

Blackbeard delighted in his attacks. In fact, he made a production of them. Just before boarding a trade ship, he tied red ribbons to his long black beard and braided slow-burning fuses into the hair, lighting the fuses with matches. Fire and smoke curled around his face, giving him the appearance of a devil. He wore daggers at his side and kept a variety of pistols strapped to his chest, loaded, cocked, and ready. Word of his monstrosity spread, prompting many a targeted captain to surrender on sight, or jump overboard. At the height of his career, Blackbeard commanded 400 pirates and four ships.

North Carolina residents were acutely aware of Blackbeard's debauchery, and they wanted it stopped. But Teach had powerful allies, such as Royal Governor Charles Eden, and his offenses went unpunished. Eventually, unable to bear the grisly tales of his conquest another day, angry locals turned to the governor of Virginia, a man by the name of Alexander

Spotswood. Lacking the men to outfit such a campaign, he made a plea to the English government, which ultimately sent Lieutenant Maynard to search for and capture or kill Blackbeard.

Maynard sailed down the Atlantic Coast, searching for the pirate's ominous black flag. He looked for days. Then, early one November morning in 1718, the crew spotted Blackbeard's ship, *Queen Anne's Revenge*, anchored among the islets. They fired a cannonball, and Blackbeard's crew fired back, tearing a hole in Maynard's vessel. Maynard and his crew ran aground on a nearby sandbar. There, they awaited the inevitable. When a fire-lit Blackbeard and his crew boarded the vessel from Virginia, Maynard and his men were prepared for combat. Daggers drawn, pistols cocked, the two forces fought a savage, bloody battle.

At last, Maynard came face to face with the pirate. He advanced, but Blackbeard was quicker. Swinging his sword across Maynard's, Blackbeard broke the lieutenant's blade in half. Maynard was helpless and stunned. With a glimmer in his eye, Blackbeard bore down upon his enemy. Just then, one of Maynard's crewmen came from behind, and with one clean swipe, beheaded the fiend. Maynard watched in awe as Blackbeard's head dropped to the deck.

The crew rejoiced over their victory and dumped the pirate's body overboard, where, according to legend, it swam three times around the ship before sinking into the dark waters of the Atlantic. As a final gesture, the crew tied Blackbeard's head to the bowsprit. It dangled off the end as a trophy and symbol of their success. For days, the ship sailed brandishing the rotting head, its black hair blowing in the wind. It was a challenge to pirates everywhere that their reign over the region was waning.

Often is this tale told on stormy nights, when the island is dark, save for the intermittent flash of the lighthouse beacon, and residents gather by their fires. There, it is whispered that, beneath the steady beam of the Ocracoke Island Light, in among the shadows of the trees, walks the headless ghost of Blackbeard; and, out across the illumined depths, his flaming vessel haunts the coast in search of its missing captain.

Ocracoke Island is accessible only by ferry. One ferry runs several times a day from Cedar Island. For further information, call 919-225-3551 or 1-800-BY-FERRY. Another ferry runs twice a day from Swan Quarter. For further information, call 252-926-1111. Another ferry runs from the southern end of Hatteras Island. This free trip takes about thirty minutes. Further information is available at 1-800-BY-FERRY.

The lighthouse is closed to the public, but visitors may walk the grounds. For additional information, visit the National Park Service Visitor Center on Ocracoke Island: Highway 12, Ocracoke, North Carolina 27960, 252-928-4531; or contact the Cape Hatteras National Seashore: Route 1, Box 675, Manteo, North Carolina 27954, 919-473-2111.

Jeremy D'Entremont

Penfield Reef Light
Near Fairfield, Connecticut

What the Reef Takes, the Reef Gives Back

Penfield Reef Light
Near Fairfield, Connecticut

A dory breezed through the Long Island Sound, rocking gently on the waves. The day was warm and quiet, except for the squall of the gulls gliding overhead and the soft sound of water lapping against the base of the boat. The vessel's occupants steered carefully toward the reef, cautiously maneuvering their boat around the rocks beneath the water's surface.

On the right, they passed the Penfield Reef Light. One of the last offshore masonry lights built, it was erected to warn sailors away from the dangerous shoals they now crossed. Knowing the area well, the two sailors picked an opportune spot for a day of fishing and anchored their vessel near the lighthouse.

The low afternoon sun cast gold-laced shadows across the water as they tossed their lines into the sea. Hoping to catch cod and flounder, maybe even a few tuna, for the evening's supper, they cast and reeled their lines back in again all afternoon. It was a perfect day for fishing, and the young fishermen were determined to fill their buckets.

As the day wore on, the two young enthusiasts lost track of time. They had caught nearly enough fish to fill the freezer, but they continued, knowing they could give the extras away to neighbors and friends.

Late in the afternoon, the weather began to turn. The gentle breeze rolled and shifted. Ominous storm clouds slid across the sky, dulling the shimmering water, and the boat began to rock among the waves.

The two young sailors were startled by the sudden change of weather. Without a second thought, they packed their belongings and pulled the anchor back onboard. They knew what they were up against.

Their fishing reef was actually a peninsula, worn down by rough and restless waters into a series of small islands. Eventually, over hundreds of years, even the islands themselves had eroded into the mile-long stretch of shoals beneath their boat—one of the most dangerous areas in the Long Island Sound.

The fishermen knew, if they didn't leave the reef immediately, they would never leave. As they pushed off, rain erupted out of the sky in sharp, stinging drops, and the small mast of the boat pitched wildly in the wind. A wave rose, casting its shadow over the side of the boat and drenching the hapless sailors. Water spilled across the floorboards and into the buckets of fish as the men struggled to steer their dory. In an instant, they lost control; the vessel spun recklessly into the rocks and capsized.

The men came up coughing, fighting to stay above the thrashing waves. Both were strong swimmers, but no match for a tempest. They were on the verge of drowning when, out of nowhere, a man appeared on the rocks near the lighthouse. Without hesitation, he swam out to the men, whose arms and legs flailed desperately in an attempt to stay afloat. The stranger grabbed one of the men and dragged him to the rocks beneath the lighthouse. Then, with equal resolve, he swam out to get the other man.

The two young fishermen lay on the rocks, weary and in shock. When they looked up to thank the man who had rescued them, he was nowhere to be seen. He had disappeared as quickly as he had appeared.

A number of local legends share themes common to this story: a shipwreck, drowning fishermen, and a small vessel too close to the rocks. In the end, the savior of all onboard appears and disappears, leaving no clues as to his identity. One similar tale involves two boys who were fishing just off the rocks in a small canoe. When their canoe flipped, and they were thrown into the choppy waters, a man appeared and dragged them to the shore of the lighthouse. The lighthouse figures prominently in each of the tales, leading many to seek answers there.

The Penfield Reef Light was built in 1874 atop a cylindrical granite pier. It was designed by renowned architect F. Hopkinson Smith, who also designed and built the lighthouse at Long Island Sound's Race Rock and laid the foundation for the Statue of Liberty. The lighthouse cost a steep sum—$55,000—and, like the Ledge Light in New London, Connecticut, it resembled a large, well-to-do home. The keeper's dwelling was attached to the 35-foot tower, whose beacon flashed 51 feet above the sea.

A two-story, four-bedroom house with an oil room, kitchen, first-floor den, and second-floor bedrooms, the dwelling was more than sufficient for a keeper and his assistant. Penfield Reef had a series of keepers over the years, including two female assistants, before the much-remembered Fredrick A. Jordan served.

On a cold December day, Jordan left the lighthouse in his small boat, bound for a Christmas holiday on the mainland. He'd made all the necessary arrangements for his leave, including last-minute cleaning and maintenance on the tower. With a final wave, he wished his assistant keeper, Rudolph Iten, happy holidays and pushed off. But just as Jordan left the lighthouse, his small boat capsized. Iten did all he could to rescue the keeper, but in the end, his efforts were fruitless. He recorded the events of the day in the keeper's log:

> Keeper left station at 12:20 PM and when about 150 yards NW of the light, his boat capsized, but he managed to cling to the overturned boat. He motioned me to lower the sailboat, but on account of the heavy seas running from the NE, it was impossible to launch the boat alone. At 1:00 PM the wind died down a bit and shifted to the south. I then lowered the boat safely and started off after the keeper who had by this time drifted about one and one half miles to the SW. When

about one-half miles from the light, the wind shifted to the SW, making a head wind and an outgoing tide which proved too much for me to pull with the heavy boat. I had to give up and returned to the station with the wind now blowing a gale from the WSW. Sent distress signals to several ships but none answered. Lost track of the keeper at 3:00 PM. He is probably lost. [sic]

Indeed, he was. Soon after 3:00 PM, Jordan's body was found adrift in the waters near the lighthouse. He had fallen victim to the very reef over which he kept his watch.

Jordan's death was the second tragedy in a month. Just weeks before his own ill-fated journey, nine barges belonging to New York's Blue Line had wrecked upon the reef, which is now known as the Blue Line Graveyard.

Since these tragedies, tales of a mysterious life-guard who saves drowning fishermen have become almost commonplace on the Long Island Sound. A spectral figure also has been seen shifting about the lighthouse. Keepers have reported seeing a form, dressed in white, floating about the lighthouse tower. At times, the form floats down the staircase and out the door, where it promptly disappears. Locals have also seen the figure in the lantern room, particularly on stormy nights, swaying in the light. On other occasions, some have caught glimpses of the shadowy spirit on the rocks at the base of the lighthouse.

It is said that Iten himself, having become keeper after Jordan's death, saw the apparition slide out of an upstairs room. As he stood watching, it made its way down the stairs and vanished. When Iten reached the first floor, he found that his journal had been placed on the table and opened to the entry recorded December 22, 1916, the day Fred Jordan died.

When asked about the ghost of Fred Jordan, Iten is said to have responded matter-of-factly, "There is an old saying, 'What the reef takes, the reef gives back.'"

The Penfield Reef Light is located in Long Island Sound, near Fairfield, Connecticut. The lighthouse can be seen from the shores of Fairfield and Bridgeport. For the optimal view, however, visitors should take a boat through the sound.

For additional information on the lighthouse, contact the Fairfield Historical Society: 636 Old Post Road, Fairfield, Connecticut 06430, 203-259-1598; fax: 203-255-2716; email: info@fairfieldhs.org. For information on boat excursions and beaches near the Penfield Reef Light, contact The Coastal Fairfield County Convention & Visitors Bureau: Merritt View, 383 Main Avenue, Norwalk, Connecticut 06851-1544, 1-800-866-7925 or 203-840-0770. Website: www.coastalct.com/home.htm

Bryan Penberthy

St. Simons Island Lighthouse
St. Simons Island, Georgia

A Keeper Reclaims His Post

St. Simons Island Lighthouse
St. Simons Island, Georgia

St. Simons Island Lighthouse towers over the entrance of St. Simons Sound just east of Brunswick, Georgia. The original lighthouse was constructed in 1808 on the very site where the colonial Fort St. Simons once stood. Built under General James Oglethorpe to protect the southern portion of the island, the fort was destroyed in 1742 by retreating soldiers during the Battle of Bloody Marsh.

At the start of the nineteenth century, a plantation owner named John Couper took possession of the land and named it Couper's Point. Because Couper supported the idea of a lighthouse, a few years later, in 1804, he sold it to the government for a dollar. It was to be the site of the island's first harbor light.

The original St. Simons Light was built of tabby—a building material composed of sand, lime, oyster shells, and water—which was taken from the remnants of nearby Fort Frederica. James Gould, the tower's chief architect, became its first keeper. President Madison appointed him to the post, at a salary of $400 a year. He served for twenty-seven years.

In 1857, the island's harbor light was raised to the rank of coastal light. But just five short years later, the 75-foot tower was reduced to rubble. In 1862, in order to prevent Federal troops from utilizing it, Confederate forces used black powder to level the lighthouse and keeper's dwelling. It took ten years and many lives to rebuild.

Finding and obtaining appropriate equipment was often difficult in post-Civil War America. It took weeks or even months to replenish needed supplies. But for the building crew of St. Simons Lighthouse, this was not the only setback. Stagnant ponds around the building site bred malaria. Several members of the construction crew, as well as the first contractor and the investor who replaced him, contracted the illness and died. On September 1, 1872, the St. Simons Lighthouse was completed under the direction of another investor. It stood 104 feet above the water.

A target for intense rains and wind, the new keeper's dwelling had been fortified with walls a foot thick. However, while these walls successfully kept the fierce storms that slam against the Georgia coast out, they were unable to quell storms brewing within.

Originally, the St. Simons Lighthouse was built as a single-family residence, but it was later converted into two separate apartments. The lighthouse keeper and his family typically shared their home with an assistant and his family. It was an ideal solution to the problem of long hours and isolation. Yet, in the case of keeper Fred Osborne and his assistant, this arrangement failed miserably.

Osborne served as keeper toward the end of the nineteenth century and was notoriously meticulous in his care—so much so, in fact, that, when the position for assistant keeper became available, there were very few applications. One gentleman, John Stevens, felt he was up to the task. He was ultimately awarded the position and trained under Osborne's tutelage. Nevertheless, Osborne never trusted him with significant duties. In retrospect, it could be said that Fred Osborne was wise not to trust John Stevens.

Unable to foster a friendship with the keeper, Stevens eventually found comfort and companionship in the keeper's wife. When Osborne found out, he flew into a rage. He confronted Stevens, and the two had a bitter and bloody argument on the front lawn of the lighthouse. Osborne pulled a pistol, but Stevens, who was carrying a shotgun, fired first.

Not wanting to face murder charges, Stevens rushed the dying Osborne to Brunswick Hospital. He told the nurses that Osborne had been shot by accident. Then, dutifully, he returned home to tend the unmanned lighthouse. Upon Osborne's death, the sheriff brought Stevens in for further questioning; but with no one else trained to tend the lighthouse, it was decided that he should return to his duties until his trial or, if necessary, until an appropriate replacement could be found. Stevens ultimately claimed self-defense, and the charges were dropped.

Prior to the murder of Fred Osborne, there had never been any indication of a ghost at the St. Simons

Island Light. Ever since, keepers, locals, and visitors have reported unusual and unexplainable activity. From 1907 until 1936, Carl Svendsen served as lighthouse keeper. When he and his family moved into the lighthouse, they had no prior knowledge of the lighthouse's haunted history. In the evenings, while preparing dinner, Mrs. Svendsen would hear sounds of footsteps walking on the staircase. Assuming it was her husband coming down for dinner, she was particularly alarmed when she realized no one was there. She shared this news with her husband, who at first thought the lonely isolation of their lighthouse life had taken its toll on his wife. But eventually, he too began to hear the footsteps.

On one occasion, Mrs. Svendsen began setting the table and heard what she thought was her husband coming down to eat. When the heavy sounds of the footsteps reached the bottom of the staircase, the kitchen door swung open and, instead of Carl, a cold wind slid through the room, frightening both Mrs. Svendsen and the family dog. The dog's fur stood on end and he began barking hysterically, as he too sensed the presence of an invisible force. The ghost never harmed the couple, and eventually, they learned to live with its presence.

Those involved with the lighthouse are hard pressed to find a reasonable explanation. Current curator, Deborah Thomas, reports that people who visit the lighthouse alone at night sometimes hear things. Most feel that Osborne's spirit returned because of unfinished business. His subordinate, John Stevens, had taken his wife, his life, and in the end, his post. Revenge was in order. But why he continued to haunt the lighthouse even after Steven's death is anyone's guess. Perhaps, as in life, he's loath to trust anyone else with its significant duties.

To reach St. Simons Island, take Interstate 95 to Highway 17. Take Highway 17 to the toll road. Maps to the island and lighthouse are available at the tollbooth.

From Brunswick, go east on the St. Simons Island causeway. Once on the island, take Kings Way to the south end of the island.

The lighthouse and Museum of Coastal History are open daily, except Mondays and some holidays. For a nominal fee, visitors may climb the tower for a magnificent view of the island, and browse through the coastal museum, which is located in the old keeper's quarters. For additional information, contact the Museum of Coastal History: P.O. Box 21136, St. Simons Island, Georgia 31522, 912-638-4666; or the Coastal Georgia Historical Society: P.O. Box 21136, St. Simons Island, Georgia 31522-0636.

John Murray

White River Light
Whitehall, Michigan

A Spirited Place

White River Light
Whitehall, Michigan

In the 1800s, industrialization started to boom in the Midwest. Charles Mears built the first sawmill on White Lake in 1838. In 1849, the Reverend William Ferry and his son, Thomas, built a water-powered sawmill at the mouth of White River, where White Lake meets Lake Michigan. Their farmed lumber went partially toward new construction in nearby Whitehall; but for the most part, it was shipped to larger cities like Chicago and Milwaukee. With an increasing number of ships transporting lumber, White River became congested, especially after the Great Chicago Fire of 1871, when lumber was in absolute demand.

As ships began to wreck more frequently, it became clear to the Michigan Legislature that a new lighthouse was needed at the entrance to White Lake. At the same time, those making their profits in the lumber industry were seeking money for the expansion of the shipping channel. Business was booming, and the lumber barons hoped to build an additional channel between White Lake and Lake Michigan.

In 1866, Congress agreed to a sum of $67,000 for the shipping channel and $10,000 for a new lighthouse at the entrance of the harbor. However, there was immediate disagreement as to the most appropriate position for the lighthouse. Construction was indefinitely halted until the channel could be built and authorities could reassess the area. It was important to position the tower where it would be most beneficial.

Work on the channel progressed slowly. In the meantime, ship captains needed a navigational aide. One shipping captain from England, William Robinson, took it upon himself to ensure the safety of his fellow sailors. He often built fires along the beach of White River to guide ships along the river.

In 1869, another $45,000 was appropriated for completion of the channel. Two years later, in 1871, it was finished. By that time, the original budget for the lighthouse had been long spent. Little more than $1,000 remained to construct a small wooden light at the end of a pier. This pier-head light guarded the new channel rather than the harbor, contrary to what ship captains had once hoped.

The faithful Captain William Robinson became the first keeper of the pier light in 1872. When the Lighthouse Board requested $4,000 for a keeper's dwelling, they were rebuffed. The next year, the board proposed a larger shore light. This time, their request was heard. In 1874, they were granted $15,000 for a new lighthouse and keeper's dwelling.

Captain Robinson and five other men assisted in the construction of the new lighthouse. Built with yellow Michigan brick and limestone blocks, the tower included a long, cast-iron staircase that ran from the cellar to the top of the tower. Robinson saw the project from start to finish and again took over his duties as keeper upon its completion.

After years of waiting, when the devoted keeper finally moved into the lighthouse with his wife, Sarah, he vowed never to leave it. The happy couple built a home in the tower, as Robinson had always envisioned, and together they raised eleven children.

Day in and day out, the keeper tended his lighthouse with wisdom and enthusiasm. He and his wife saw to the maintenance of the tower and home, raised their children, and made it their personal mission in life to protect ships along the shores of White River. Life was good. They were very much in love with one another and perfectly fulfilled by their duties. They imagined a long, happy life together in the lighthouse, but it was not to be. Sarah died suddenly at the age of fifty-eight. Robinson was unprepared for such a loss and inconsolable. To keep his spirits up, he concentrated all of his energies on the care of the lighthouse.

As the keeper grew older and nearer the age of retirement, his grandson and assistant, Captain William Bush, took over as keeper. The captain, however, was reluctant to loose his grip on the White River Light. Even though government regulation allowed only one lighthouse keeper and his family to reside in the lighthouse at a time, Robinson refused to leave. Out of respect, Bush deferred to his grandfather's seniority and allowed the captain to remain in the house and tend to the beacon as he had always done. Though the tower technically belonged to his grandson, Robinson carried out most of the work until well into his eighties.

After many years of this arrangement, it was a well-known fact, even to the Lighthouse Board, that

Robinson was still residing and working in the lighthouse. In 1915, the board insisted that the keeper
retire from his duties and the house. At eighty-seven,
Robinson was no longer deemed capable of tending
the light. He walked with a cane and couldn't get
around as well as he once did, which made him a lia-
bility. They wanted Bush, a much younger and more
capable man, permanently on duty. Robinson was
unmoved. To the dismay of the organization, he
refused to abandon the light.

At this point, the board realized that significant
measures would have to be taken. They never got the
chance. Determined to live out his last years in the
home he'd shared with his beloved wife, Captain
Robinson died less than two weeks after their
decree—and still he didn't leave. The ghost of Captain
William Robinson has been a constant presence at
the White River Light since the hour of his death.

Today, Karen McDonnell serves as director and
curator, tending to the lighthouse. A self-described
skeptic, she lived in the lighthouse for two years
before experiencing any of the phenomena described
to her by her predecessors. "By that time, I had dis-
missed it," she says. "Then I began to hear the footsteps on the stairs." Always between the hours of
2:00 and 4:00 AM, McDonnell heard the sound of
footsteps, accompanied by the sound of a cane,
steadily climbing the stairs. "There's really no explanation, not wind or anything, that would create that
sound pattern of someone walking with a cane," she
explains. "So, I had a hard time dismissing it."

Once the captain had introduced himself to the
new keeper, his wife was soon to follow. However,

before that could happen, McDonnell had to make a change. Feeling that the devoted wife of the light-house's longest keeper ought to be remembered as well, McDonnell tracked down a portrait of Sarah Robinson and hung it on the wall beside one of the captain. Since then, she's noticed unexplained behavior that previous curators never mentioned. Putting two and two together, she's come to attribute this behavior to none other than the captain's wife.

"For one thing," McDonnell says, "the pictures that hang in the hallway, the pictures of the captain and Sarah, always go askew in different directions. If it were the wind, or something like that moving them, it would be a uniform movement, not this way and that."

Another time, McDonnell encountered an even more significant clue as to the spirit's identity. She got some help with a household chore. "I was dusting a glass display case, when the phone rang," she explains. "I went to answer the phone and left everything as it was. I have a photographic memory; so, when I got back, I noticed that the rag had been moved and a whole section of the case, which had been dusty when I left, had been cleaned. I don't know why, but I felt that that was definitely Sarah's doing."

Over the years, McDonnell's affection for the couple has grown. "I've just always felt that theirs was a great love story," she says, "and I'm not the only one who feels that way either. "One day, a young professor who visited the lighthouse with a group of students substantiated her opinion about the Robinsons. "He was taking a bunch of students up the peninsula in a boat," McDonnell says. "The lighthouse was not on their itinerary at all. But when he saw it, he was absolutely riveted. He decided he had to see it. So, on the spur of the moment, the group docked its boat at the yacht club—a good mile and a half away—and walked to the lighthouse! After they'd toured the place, the professor asked me if I'd ever sensed a presence there. I told him that, yes, I had. Then he told me that he'd seen an image, like a flash in his mind, of a couple, obviously very much in love, sitting in one of the [recessed] windows. Later, he and his fiancé came back and had their picture taken in front of that window."

There is little doubt that the devoted lighthouse keeper, Captain William Robinson, and his wife, Sarah, remain in the lighthouse, but you won't hear Karen McDonnell say that they "haunt" the premises. "I don't like to say that the place is haunted," she muses, "because the word 'haunted' brings to mind dark and frightening things. I like to say that it is 'spirited.' This is a spirited place."

Take U.S. 31 to the White Lake Drive exit. Turn right off the exit onto White Lake Drive. Go several miles until the road dead ends at South Shore Drive. Turn left onto South Shore Drive and continue on, bearing to the right after the stop sign. Continue on to the next stop sign where South Shore Drive joins Murray Road. Follow Murray Road approximately one mile, and the museum will be to the left. It is open from the beginning of June through the end of September and by appointment during the off-season. For additional information, contact the museum at 6199 Murray Road, Whitehall, Michigan 49461, 231-894-8265; email: curator@whiteriverlightstation.org

New London Ledge Light
New London, Connecticut

The Light, the Keeper, His Wife, and Her Lover

New London Ledge Light
New London, Connecticut

What could be more chilling than a haunted mansion floating above a reckless sea? Here, at the entrance to New London Harbor, sits a grand three-story lighthouse in the French Second-Empire style. With eleven rooms, the house exhibits the grace, sophistication, and opulence of homes along the Connecticut coast. This was by design. Wealthy homeowners on the coast demanded that the building blend in with its surroundings. Constructed at the start of the twentieth century of red brick and granite with a mansard roof, New London Ledge was a jewel among lighthouses—one of few not built of cast iron. Any keeper would have been proud to call it home.

Lit in 1909, the New London Ledge Light was one of the last lighthouses built in New England. Its sister light, the New London Harbor Light, had been one of the first. Lit in 1760, the New London Harbor Light had begun as one of only three lights illuminating the coastline in colonial America. Its 90-foot tower was designed to warn sailors away from rocky shoals in the harbor. Yet, tragically, sailing vessels continued to wreck against jagged shoals at the mouth of the Thames River. The light simply didn't reach that far. For many years, sailors complained of this dark and treacherous stretch, but it wasn't until 1890, nearly a century and a half later, that statesmen began lobbying for an additional lighthouse. Then, it was another nineteen years before the New London Ledge Light was built—and for the astronomical sum of $93,968.

Built by New London's Hamilton R. Douglas Company, the Ledge Light was truly an island unto itself. A timber crib had been towed 12 miles upstream, sunk on top a 200-foot-long shoal and filled with concrete. An 18-foot-tall pier had been constructed on top of this foundation, and the house, in turn, had been constructed on the pier. From a distance, the structure seemed to float among the waves.

For lighthouse keepers and their families, life was a lonely and isolated existence in the middle of the ocean. Thick fog slides through the harbor and eerily wraps around the dwelling. Loud, swelling waves crash against the base of the lighthouse. And the only way in or out of the lighthouse for keepers and their families was by boat. The conditions left little to be desired, especially during inclement weather. The threat of flooding winds and rain instilled fear in any keeper who ever lived through a massive storm.

Especially difficult were times when harsh winter storms would blow in for days. As long as the storm persisted, keepers and their families were forced to remain indoors, and the lighthouse became a place of insufferable confinement. One hurricane, which occurred in 1938, created waves so fierce they were as high as the second-story windows. Keepers and their families were forced to watch the rough waters slam against their home and could only hope the windows wouldn't break before the storm subsided.

Even when days were pleasant, those who tended the lighthouse were housebound unless they took leave and went inland. Getting outdoors for a walk was confined to small strolls around the deck. The isolation was enough to drive the average person out of his mind.

In 1936, a young man moved in to tend the lighthouse. Day in, day out, the new keeper worked hard to keep the lighthouse in perfect working order; he swabbed the decks, polished the brass, cleaned the stately building, and tended the light. However content the new keeper was, this was not the life his young bride had dreamed of. She lived alone in the town, kept away from her husband for days, sometimes weeks on end. Eventually, the monotony and seclusion began to torment the young bride. But the keeper was loyal to his job. He didn't want to resign.

Inevitably, the young wife began to resent her husband and her life of isolation. Seeking companionship, she ran off to seek a more adventurous life with the captain of the Block Island ferry. From then on, her husband felt firsthand the isolation of which she'd so often spoken.

Shortly after his wife's departure, the keeper was found dead of an apparent suicide. Some believed that he had jumped from the catwalk surrounding the lantern gallery. Others said that he had been so distraught by his misfortune that he lost his concentration and fell. All agreed that his pretty young wife had led to his ruin.

Today, his ghost, who's come to be known as Ernie, haunts the New London Ledge Light. One keeper claimed that Ernie called out his name as he descended a ladder. Others have spotted his likeness at the top of the stairs. In some ways, Ernie seems to be tending to the only thing in life that never disappointed him—his faithful mansion light. On good days, he has been known to polish brass and swab the decks. In other ways, he seems as distraught as he must have been on the night he died. Bad days find him leaving tools lying about, setting boats adrift, turning televisions and foghorns on and off, opening and closing doors, and rearranging books on shelves.

In 1939, the United States Coast Guard assumed control of the lighthouse. Its crews tended the light until 1987, when it became automated. The day before automation, a Coast Guardsman summed up his opinion of the Ledge Light in the keeper's log: "Rock of slow torture. Ernie's domain. Hell on earth? May New London Ledge's light shine on forever because I'm through. I will watch it from afar while drinking a brew." Clearly, not everyone can cope with the isolation of the New London Ledge Light. But even in death, Ernie remains loyal to the post he did not want to resign.

New London Ledge Light is located at the mouth of the Thames River and is accessible only by boat. For further information, contact New London Ledge Lighthouse Foundation: P.O. Box 855, New London, Connecticut 06320, 860-442-2222. Cruises and walking tours are available mid-June through the end of August and are conducted through the New London Ledge Lighthouse Foundation. Reservations are strongly recommended, as space is limited. For online information, log on to www.oceanology.org

The Block Island Ferry also offers cruises to the lighthouse from mid-June through Labor Day. For ferry information, call 203-442-7891.

Bryan Penberthy

Alcatraz Island Lighthouse
Alcatraz Island, California

A Light In the Darkness

Alcatraz Island Lighthouse
Alcatraz Island, California

Otherwise known as The Rock, Alcatraz prison has housed some of the country's most dangerous convicts. Today, the spirits of these iniquitous criminals still haunt the island. Thieves, rapists, military deserters, serial murderers, gangsters, and outlaws have served time here, and some say their evil energy still exists.

In the early 1850s, when ships arrived daily for the California Gold Rush, government officials saw the need for a series of lighthouses. Because the bay was difficult to enter and ships often wrecked into the island, the Alcatraz Island Lighthouse, resembling a two-story California cottage with a tower in the middle, became the first active light on the Pacific Coast.

A fog bell was added in 1856.

Named *La Isla de los Alcatraces*, or "The Island of the Pelicans," by Spanish explorer Juan Manuel de Ayala in 1775, Alcatraz was once barren, with little vegetation. Flocks of pelicans soared about the small

island, peaceful in its isolation. In the early nineteenth century, the United States Army took notice of
its isolation. In its estimation, the island was the ideal
location for a military fortress. Rough currents and
poor weather conditions hindered access to the
island, which commanded a strategic view of San
Francisco. About the time the lighthouse was erected,
the military began building its fortress to prevent
enemy ships from entering the bay. It added a wharf
for supplies and built storehouses, roadways, bar-
racks, and a number of offices.

In 1859, a group of men was locked in the basement room of the guardhouse for unexplained crimes.
The men's crimes went unrecorded in army files;
however, their incarceration became significant in the
island's history. They were to be the first in a long line
of prisoners. By the summer of 1861, Alcatraz
became the official military prison for the Department
of the Pacific, housing Civil War prisoners and
Confederate sympathizers caught celebrating
Abraham Lincoln's murder.

In the early years, prison conditions were
deplorable. Men were packed into cold, filthy cells
and forced to sleep almost on top of one another.
There was no running water or heat, and inadequate
plumbing. Over the next forty years, the prison grew
and crowded out the lighthouse, which met its end in
1906. An earthquake leveled San Francisco that year
and extensively damaged the lighthouse. Longtime
keeper B.F. Leeds was present during the quake. Like
many who experienced the disaster, he thought the
end of the world had come—a reasonable conclusion
considering his surroundings. Afterward, the dam-

aged light was torn down, and a new lighthouse was commissioned. It took three years to complete the 84-foot concrete tower. It was powered by electricity, but a keeper was still needed to man it and service fog signals on the north and south ends of the island.

The life of a keeper on Alcatraz Island was bleak. With the living quarters so close to the prison, keepers had to use extreme caution when going about their daily activities. Their children, who attended school in San Francisco, rode across the grounds in a guard bus. Then, a prison boat transported them across the bay. Keepers' wives followed the same precautions whenever they had to leave the island. What's more, all outgoing and incoming passengers were counted to ensure that there were no stowaways. The families of keepers had to endure this indignity as often as twice a day. For their own safety, every aspect of their lives was regimented in this way. Even their trash was confiscated. It had to be crushed and dumped into the waters off the island to prevent prisoners from acquiring materials for weapons.

A keeper's duties were equally regimented. For example, when the fog signals needed servicing and the keeper had to cross to the other side of the island, the prison went on lock-down. No prisoner was allowed in the compound as the keeper crossed. The entire operation was carried out with the utmost caution and secrecy. The guards gave secret hand signals as a way of communicating the keeper's progress from gate to gate.

During the Great Depression, a wave of crime swept across America, and the population at Alcatraz boomed. The prison housed several of the age's well-known criminals. Included among the residents were Al Capone, George "Machine Gun" Kelly, Alvin Karpis, and Arthur "Doc" Barker.

By 1933, the Federal Bureau of Prisons had taken over The Rock; and by 1934, it had established a maximum-security prison. It was indeed, as originally intended, a fortress. Guards lined the grounds with machine guns, and barbed-wire fences punctuated the perimeter. Even the lighthouse keeper, isolated within his concrete watchtower, must have felt imprisoned in these new surroundings. Like the inmates, who by this time had nicknamed the prison "Hellcatraz," he suffered greatly from the monotony and loneliness. From his tower, he could see the bustling port, party boats, trade ships, and glowing city lights. Ironically, the Alcatraz Island Light afforded an enviable view of life in San Francisco. But everything about the life of a keeper on Alcatraz Island was decidedly unenviable—especially his view of the depravity below.

On May 2, 1946, the keeper had a bird's eye view when inmate Bernard Coy escaped. He killed a guard and secured weapons before freeing his five accomplices. The Marines were called in to restore order, and in no time, the fugitives hit a massive roadblock. They couldn't open the gate that led into the recreation yard. For close to two days, the lighthouse keeper watched in horror as the trapped prisoners waged a bloody battle against guards and Marines. After an apocalyptic fight, three of the six escapees were dead, as well as a number of guards. The lighthouse keeper later described the standoff as "44 hours of hell."

After more than half a century of hell on the "Island of Devils," keepers, guards, and inmates alike were liberated from its shores. In 1963, the lighthouse was automated and the penitentiary closed. Six years later, the lighthouse mysteriously burned, leaving the keeper's dwelling in ruins.

With such a dark and haunted history, Alcatraz was destined to remain a topic of profound interest. Today, curious travelers flock to see it, hoping to experience some of its horror firsthand. The D cellblock, also known as "solitary," is a particularly popular tourist attraction. Said to be the most haunted area on the island, to this day, it remains colder than any of the other cellblocks. Psychics and ghost hunters have reported intense paranormal activity here, and visitors have reported feeling cold, tingling sensations in their arms and fingers. The sounds of screams, rattling metal, and marching footsteps have also been heard here, and many have sensed the presence of evil spirits.

In the 1940s, legend had it that "The Hole," a dark, cold, windowless room in cellblock D, was haunted by an evil spirit. Prisoners feared isolation in The Hole because a pair of glowing eyes reportedly glared at them in the darkness. Inmates and guards had often seen a man dressed in nineteenth-century clothing wandering the corridors of D-block late at night. They speculated that perhaps he was the evil presence whose eyes shone out in The Hole.

One night, as was often the case, an inmate who had been confined to the dark cell began screaming. The guards jeered and laughed, assuming that the ghost story had gotten the better of him. All night he screamed, and all night his screams went unheeded. By morning, his cries had subsided. When the guards opened the cell, the man lay strangled, finger marks around his neck. Autopsy reports showed that the inmate could not have strangled himself; another force had to have been present in the cell. The news spread like wildfire: the evil spirit with the glowing eyes had claimed its first victim.

The following day, guards lined up the prisoners in cellblock D for a head count and came up extra. To their dismay, the murdered inmate stood in the line as usual. The block went silent, and everyone stared at the man, aghast. Within moments, the ghost vanished without a trace.

A dark energy ricochets off the walls of Alcatraz still. Repugnant odors sift through the salty air, mixing with the sea spray and fog. Wailing sobs, low moans, and piercing screams can be heard on the breeze. Apparitions of ex-prisoners and guards have appeared to visitors and rangers alike, and all who visit are left with a sense of unrest. The only benevolent spirit on the island is that of the original lighthouse, which is said to appear in times of intense fog, accompanied by a loud whistle and a flashing green light. Perhaps, just as it used to warn sailors of the island's dark shore, the lighthouse now warns visitors of the island's dark past.

Alcatraz Island Lighthouse is located in San Francisco Bay. Now part of the Golden Gate National Recreation Area, the National Park Service offers various prison exhibits, self-guided walks, orientation videos with historical footage, and interpretive talks given by park rangers. Various portions of Alcatraz, including the Alcatraz Island Lighthouse, are closed to the public. Visitors may walk the grounds of the lighthouse.

Alcatraz Island also offers impressive views of San Francisco, as well as a pleasant nature trail. The Agave trail starts on the east side of the island near the ferryboat landing, winds through a protected bird sanctuary, and ends on the southern tip of the island near the parade ground. The trail is open from late September to mid-February.

Ferry rides to the island are available year-round on the Blue and Gold Fleet, a concessionaire of the National Park Service. Tickets are sold with or without an audio tour and range in price according to age. Tours to the island depart from Pier 41 at Fisherman's Wharf in San Francisco. Evening tours are also available on a limited basis and feature sunset and evening cityscape views. For advance tickets, call 415-705-5555 or order tickets online at www.blueandgoldfleet.com For more information, call 415-773-1188.

Florida Keys National
Marine Sanctuary

Carysfort Reef Lighthouse
Key Largo, Florida

A Tale of Two Keepers

Carysfort Reef Lighthouse
Key Largo, Florida

The sparkling, emerald waters off Florida's most southern tip hide an ocean floor littered with the skeletal remains of ships. Here, a number of factors work against safe passage. During hurricane season, driving winds and rain pound across the open waters of Key Largo. Sudden squalls have thrown many a sailor spinning into the wild, storm-driven seas. Moreover, just off Key Largo lies a vast and dangerous stretch of reef. In 1695, the *TMS Winchester*, a 60-gun ship, met its ruin on the reef. Seventy-five years later, on October 23, 1770, the *HMS Carysfort* wrecked on the same stretch. Afterward, the reef became known as Carysfort Reef. In 1824, Congress allocated $20,000 for the building of a lightship in the area. At that time, no one knew of a way to build a sound structure on the reef itself, one capable of surviving the force of the turbulent sea. Even lightships in the area proved to be no match for the rough, choppy waters around the reef. Five short years later, the first lightship, *Caesar*, had already fallen prey to the elements. Its replacement, the lightship *Florida*, eventually met with some trouble of its own.

The largest of the Florida Keys, Key Largo extends 30 miles from end to end and was originally called *Cayo Lago*, or "Long Island," by the Spanish. Pirates and smugglers once used the island as a base of operations. Many believe, however, that the Indians were its first inhabitants. As settlers moved into Florida, the Seminoles became especially protective of their land. In a well-documented strike, they attacked and extinguished the light of the Cape Florida Lighthouse.

For some time, the lightship in Carysfort Reef had a significant presence, as it was one of few navigational aids for miles. A blow to it was a blow to Florida's citizens. Thus, like the Cape Florida Lighthouse, it was a logical target. On June 26, 1837, the Seminoles launched an attack.

Friends were visiting Captain John Walton and his crew aboard the *Florida* that day. Wanting to prepare an adequate meal for his guests, Walton had decided to go inland and gather vegetables from a garden he kept onshore. As the vessel approached, the Seminoles watched from the shore of Key Largo, prepared to strike. Just as the vessel docked, they charged, shooting the captain and his crew. Walton and one other man died instantly. Three other men, two of whom were wounded, narrowly escaped.

As it turned out, the lightship was of as little help to other seamen on the reef as it had been to Captain Walton and his crew. As a strategic presence, it drew too much attention to itself; as a navigational aid, it didn't draw enough. From 1833 to 1841, despite the ship's constant vigilance, more than 60 vessels were lost on the reef. Finally, in 1848, Congress appropriated funds for a masonry tower. Notable lighthouse builder Winslow Lewis submitted the first plans; however, there were delays in the building, and his plans were never fulfilled. In 1852, America's new Lighthouse Board chose plans submitted by Lewis' nephew, Isaiah W.P. Lewis. These plans called for an iron-pile lighthouse.

Having invented a new method for securing reef lighthouses to the coral rock beneath, Captain Howard Stansbury started the project. When the foundation had been laid, construction halted. The project met with delays, and when it was time to start up again, Stansbury was indisposed. A new contractor had to be obtained. The project endured two such replacements before its completion on March 10, 1852. The beacon towered 100 feet above the high-water mark.

Living in an offshore, iron-pile lighthouse was a unique experience to say the least. High winds cut against the iron poles. Rough waters rushed through the stilted base. Heavy rains washed over the glass enclosure at the top, eliminating visibility. In short, conditions were severe. Among other things, keeping adequate food supplies proved difficult. With no means of refrigeration, food was kept cool in the water below the lighthouse; but as Florida waters are relatively warm, it spoiled within a couple of days. Denied even the pleasure of a wholesome meal, keepers were forced to rely on canned food. In all respects, the situation was far from ideal. Yet, true to form, a series of loyal keepers tended the Carysfort

Reef Lighthouse until the 1970s, when solar panels were installed. More amazing than their devotion in the face of such discomfiture was their devotion in the face of Captain Charles M. Johnson. Keepers also had to put up with the ghost of this former lightship captain who had died during his short service.

The cantankerous Captain Johnson died just after the lighthouse was lit, to the sorrow of no one. Generally regarded as a heathen, he was despised by his assistants. In truth, they were relieved to see him go. However, it seems they were destined not to be so easily rid of him. After his death, his disquieting presence continued to plague keepers and their assistants. Deep, guttural groans rolled through the rafters. These sounds began soft and low, growing louder as the hours passed and the night grew old. Eventually, they intensified to high-pitched, human-sounding screams. Needless to say, on top of everything else, it was hard to get a good night's sleep in the Carysfort Reef Lighthouse.

Some now attribute the scary noises to the joints in Isaiah Lewis' iron plating. Of course, those who knew Captain Johnson were certain that it was he who roamed the halls. He had never been the type to rest in peace—or, as his assistants well knew, to allow anyone else the pleasure.

Carysfort Reef Lighthouse is located off-shore, about six miles from Key Largo and about twelve miles from the John Pennekamp Coral Reef State Park headquarters. The tower is closed to visitors, and the shallow reef makes it difficult to take a boat to the base.

Hendricks Head Light Station
Boothbay Harbor, Maine

The Infant and the Lady of Dusk

Hendricks Head Light Station
Boothbay Harbor, Maine

Hendricks Head Lighthouse sits on a rocky, windswept shore on the east side of the Sheepscot River, six miles from Boothbay Harbor. Biting winter gales and towering, storm-driven waves have sent many an unfortunate soul into the razor-like ledges of Hendricks Head. At the start of the nineteenth century, these perilous waters were nearly impassable. As a remedy to the situation, the first Hendricks Head Lighthouse was built in 1829; it was replaced in 1875 with the existing tower.

Like many coastal towns in Maine, Hendricks Head boasts a wealth of legends and lore. These legends have been passed down over the years, told and retold on winter nights to wide-eyed children. One such story involves a much-disputed shipwreck.

According to the tale, in March of 1870, lighthouse keeper Jaruel Marr and his wife, Catherine, stood huddled together, watching helplessly as the tumultuous Atlantic assaulted a wayward vessel. A whirling snowstorm blinded the captain of the ship and

obstructed his view of the lighthouse. He was danger-
ously close to the rocks on Hendricks Head. Marr
knew the vessel was in trouble as large waves drove
it closer and closer to a dangerous stretch of shoals.

Debating whether his small dory would make it
the half-mile out to the ship, the keeper crawled down
to the rocky edge of the water to check conditions.
He realized then that the waves were too intense, the
winds too brutal, and the air too cold. From this van-
tage point, he could see that all those aboard the
unfortunate ship were getting washed over by the
pounding waves. The water froze on impact with the
ship, and crewmembers were becoming encased in a
layer of ice. Marr knew his small dory was no match
for the waves. Much to his despair, he was resigned
to wait, hoping for a lull in the storm.

Together, the Marrs stood watching the hapless
ship well into the night. As the gray sky faded to
black, they lit a large bonfire on the beach, hoping to
encourage anyone still alive to hang on. Not long
afterward, the couple noticed a large bundle bobbing
over the waves. Marr crawled down to the edge of
the water and reeled it in with a boat hook. To his
dismay, he realized he had rescued two feather mat-
tresses. He scrutinized the bundle to see if there was
something he could have missed. Then, it dawned on
him: something must have been sent between them.
Quickly he cut the ropes and found a box. Sure
enough, inside the box was a baby girl. Miraculously,
she was still alive.

Marr gathered the baby up and held her close to
his chest. He and Catherine ran with the crying infant
up to the keeper's cottage. There, Catherine took the

baby into the house, bundled her in warm blankets, and rocked her by the fire. Marr returned to the beach to send a signal to the ship. He was determined to let those still alive know that he had received their package. Later, when the storm let up, he could no longer see the ship; it had been ravaged by the sea. Soon after, wreckage began to wash ashore. The saddened keeper examined the remnants of the ship that he had been unable to save. Before long, he came upon the box that had borne the child. In it, he found blankets, a small locket, and a note from the baby's mother, commending her soul to God.

The Marrs already had five children of their own and couldn't afford another. Nevertheless, they took it upon themselves to find a home for the orphaned baby. They were delighted when a doctor and his wife, summer residents at Hendricks Head, came forth to claim the child.

Extensive arguments have been made to discredit this account, but word has it that Marr's great-great-granddaughter, Elisa Trepanier, validated the story, claiming she'd heard it spoken of all her life. She even knew the baby's name: Seaborne. Fact or fiction, the legend of the rescued baby remains a favorite among lighthouse enthusiasts.

Another favorite legend, passed down for more than seventy years, is that of the "Lady of Dusk." One cold December day in 1931, an unaccompanied woman took a bus into Boothbay Harbor. She wore a smart, black dress. As the bus, filled mostly with locals, rumbled into town, she sat poised and made no conversation. When the bus stopped in the harbor, she climbed off, carrying only a small suitcase.

The afternoon was warmer than usual for December in Maine, but still cold by most standards. Wind rolled lightly across the jagged, naked branches of the trees. The sun hung low in the sky and cast shadows across summer cottages that would remain locked until well into spring. Waves spilled across the deserted beach.

The woman walked through town with her head held high, before slipping inside the Fullerton Hotel and asking politely for a room. The clerk nodded, assuming the woman was in town on business or perhaps to purchase summer property. Giving the woman a key, he wished her a pleasant stay.

Once upstairs, the woman unlocked her suitcase. She freshened up from her trip but didn't rest. Apparently, she had somewhere to be. Moments later, she let herself out of her room and locked the door behind her. Back in the lobby, she slipped past the desk and out the front door. On the street, she came upon some passersby and asked them to point her in the direction of the open ocean. They suggested she visit the wharf, which offered the most charming view in Boothbay Harbor. Showing little interest in the view, she thanked them just the same and went on her way, continuing up the looping road that wound around the harbor to Southport and Hendricks Head.

By this time, the delicate wind had picked up. It rose and fell and was at times still, at times quite restless. Dark clouds pushed across the low afternoon sun, and a threat of snow loomed on the horizon. The dignified woman didn't seem to notice or care. She continued with long, determined strides up the road to Southport. Mrs. Pinkham, who ran the Southport

Post Office, was outside locking up for the evening when the woman passed. Her husband, Charlie, was finalizing the day's sales in his general store and overheard their conversation.

The woman saw Mrs. Pinkham and stopped to ask for directions to the ocean. Naturally, Mrs. Pinkham pointed her to the stretch of shore directly across the highway. The woman nodded, obviously aware of the ocean's proximity. But instead of moving on, she inquired again about a particular sweep of ocean. Confused, Mrs. Pinkham suggested Hendricks Head. The woman nodded. She seemed familiar with the name and wished for directions there. Knowing the sun would soon sink below the horizon and concerned with the weather, Mrs. Pinkham warned her against taking the lonely road to Hendricks Head that night. But the woman couldn't be bothered. She thanked Mrs. Pinkham and went on her way. As the clouds slid over the sun, Mrs. Pinkham watched the woman fade into the distance. She could see her black dress flapping in the wind as her long hair tossed behind her.

When his wife came in from the cold, Mr. Pinkham questioned her about the mysterious woman. Who was she, and where was she going? Why was she so determined to reach Hendricks Head in the dark? Mrs. Pinkham told him of the woman's intentions, but he wasn't satisfied. He felt uneasy about the whole affair.

Alone, the woman continued up the sandy path until she heard someone approaching. Not wanting to be warned away again, she slipped into the trees and watched quietly as Charles Knight, the keeper of the Hendricks Head Lighthouse, passed on his way to the post office. When he was a good distance from her, the woman stepped out of her hiding place and continued her journey.

Back in town, the Pinkhams told Knight about the strange woman heading to his part of the island and asked whether he had passed her along the way. Knight was perplexed. He'd seen no one on his way into town. The whole story was extremely curious. What could warrant so dangerous an excursion? Vowing to look for her on his return, Knight wished the Pinkhams a good evening and set out. He wanted to overtake the woman before it got dark.

Knight grew more and more apprehensive as darkness began to cover the island. With the thick clouds hovering overhead, it was becoming almost too dark to see. Having walked the route time and again, Knight had no trouble finding his way home, but he was nervous for the woman. She didn't know the way.

As he approached the lighthouse, he saw a figure dart behind one of the summer cottages. Sure it was the woman the Pinkhams had told him about, he called out but received no answer. Again, he called. And again, no answer came. By the time he reached the summer cottage, whoever it had been was gone.

The woman never returned to the Fullerton Hotel that evening, and by morning, everyone in Southport was uneasy about her mysterious disappearance. Willis Brewer, a fisherman in the area, agreed to go look for her. He retraced her steps from the Southport Post Office to Hendricks Head. He discovered the place where she stepped off the road as Charles Knight passed and found her trail to the summer cottages. He followed her steps west, but upon reaching the water, found nothing. For days, the mystery remained unsolved.

Almost a week later, on Sunday, December 6, Charlie Pinkham, who volunteered at the firehouse, gathered a couple of men and headed down to the waters below the lighthouse. They scanned the open sweep of the ocean but saw nothing. Finally, one of the firemen caught a glimpse of something bobbing in the water. The undertow had pulled the body of the woman up to the surface. When they pulled her in, they discovered that a flatiron had been tied to her body in order to weigh her down. Rumors spread of the woman's suicide, but there were some who suspected foul play.

Southport authorities conducted an extensive background search, but unfortunately, the woman had left nothing to be overturned. Her suitcase in the hotel had not a trace of identification. Detectives arrived from New York City. Reporters from all over ran stories. The Missing Persons Bureau checked time and again for leads, but in the end, no one came forward to claim her. In January 1932, she was buried in the cemetery along the road to Hendricks Head. No headstone marked her grave.

For years after the incident, an unidentified black limousine was seen in the area on the anniversary of her death. To add further mystery to the story, locals began seeing the ghost of a woman in black wandering the area around Hendricks Head Lighthouse. Upon closer inspection, they found footprints in the sand but no other trace of her. Known as the Lady of Dusk, she is often seen roaming the beach near the lighthouse in the early evening. She's also been seen on the stretch of road between Boothbay Harbor and Hendricks Head. It's even been rumored that she walks dignified, steadfast, and determined toward the water, just as she did on the night she drowned.

The mystery is still a hotly debated topic of conversation in Hendricks Head, Maine. Locals and visitors alike enjoy speculating as to the cause of the woman's death. Some have suggested that she lost her family fortune during the stock market crash and was unable to face a life of poverty. Others assert that the woman was in mourning and sought solace in the deep, dark waters. One far-fetched argument goes so far as to claim that she was involved in liquor smuggling and had crossed the wrong people. But for all their speculations, no one knows for sure what befell the Lady of Dusk that night, or why she darts among the cottages, beneath the soft glow of the Hendricks Head Light. She remains as elusive and mysterious in death as she was in life.

Hendricks Head is privately owned. Visitors are not permitted near the lighthouse. In fact, "no trespassing" signs warn visitors away from the entrance to the driveway. A zoom lens is necessary to take photos of the lighthouse. There is a small beach in West Southport that offers a view of it, but the best way to see the tower is by boat. Commercial tours are available out of Boothbay harbor. Cruises to a variety of Maine lighthouses, including Hendricks Head, are available through the Maine Maritime Museum, 207-443-1316.

For additional information, contact the Boothbay Region Historical Society: P.O. Box 272, Boothbay Harbor, Maine 04538-0272, 207-633-0820; Website: www.boothbayhistorical.org

Jeremy D'Entremont

Owl's Head Lighthouse
Owl's Head, Maine

Heroism and Hauntings

Owl's Head Lighthouse
Owl's Head, Maine

Just where Owl's Head got its name, no one is entirely sure. It's been suggested that the jagged promontory, named *Medacut* by the Indians, resembles an owl: two hollows in the rock form the shape of eyes, and a small ridge juts out like a beak. Despite this explanation, few here see anything but rugged terrain, pine trees, and a few spruce trees at the top near the lighthouse.

The great height of Owl's Head allows the 30-foot lighthouse, built in 1825, to tower 100 feet above the water. The rocks below are razor-like, the waters rough, and the storms fierce. Not surprisingly, before the lighthouse was built, as well as after, the area bore witness to innumerable shipwrecks.

During the bleak days of winter, when the sky fades to white and the clouds grow thick with snow, locals retell the tales of fearless sailors and the loyal lighthouse keepers and their assistants who served here. Then they speak in hushed tones of the phantom at Owl's Head Light.

The Tale of the Fearless Sailor

During a brutal December storm of 1850, five ships were trapped in the freezing waters off Maine's rocky coast. All five had been tossed off course and into the shoreline. As the temperatures plummeted well below zero, the salt spray of the waves froze as soon as it hit the vessels. Inches of ice encased each ship, making it impossible to escape.

That same night, a ship headed for Boston was docked at Jameson's Port, an area close to Owl's Head. With no explanation to his crew of three—seaman Roger Elliott, mate Richard Ingraham, and Lydia Dyer, Ingraham's fiancée—the captain climbed off the boat and never returned. To this day, no one knows why he left. He may have been troubled by the storm and sought news in town. There, he may have learned of the five lost ships and lost heart. Or, as many believe, he may have had a premonition about the fate of his own ship and simply fled.

The winds howled that night, and the snow blew with fury, but the loyal crew patiently awaited the return of their captain. To keep warm, they huddled together, listening to the assault of the waves. Their boat rocked recklessly in the raging surf, straining the cables that held the ship at port. Inevitably, these cables snapped, sending the boat and its crew careening across Penobscot Bay toward the rocky ledges of Owl's Head. The schooner hit sharp rocks and its base was shattered, but somehow, the decks remained above water. Freezing waves crashed upon the ship with savage force. There was no way off the boat. With each passing second, the crew grew more and more horrified. They huddled under a wool blanket beneath the weight of the ice that was mounting on top.

Eventually, the ice cut off the oxygen inside their tent, and Lydia and Ingraham fell unconscious. Roger Elliott spent the night picking away at the ice with a sheath knife, working to maintain a small air hole. By morning, the storm had calmed. Exhausted and desperate, Roger Elliott used his fists to break free from the block of ice that had formed around them during the night.

As water kicked the boat against the edge of the rocks, Elliot jumped. He managed to climb onto a landing and pull himself up a steep precipice. Steadily he climbed up the slippery, ice-covered rocks to shore and found the road to the lighthouse. He'd seen its light from the port and knew that someone would be tending it.

Remarkably, lighthouse keeper William Masters came upon the disheveled seaman in the road. He gathered the stranger up in his sleigh and took him back to the lighthouse. Inside, Masters got Elliott into some warm clothes and served him hot rum. Before passing out, Elliott managed to tell the keeper about the two crewmembers he'd left behind on the boat.

Masters sprung into action. He gathered twelve men, and together they headed for the wreck site. The search crew quickly located the schooner and climbed aboard. There they found the young couple lying frozen under a block of ice. Believing them dead, Masters lost heart. But he refused to leave them within their icy coffin. He insisted that the men thaw the ice and work to retrieve the bodies. For hours, the rescue crew chipped away at the ice. Finally, they pulled the blue and lifeless bodies of Lydia Dyer and Richard Ingraham from the ship.

Inspired by this small success, the group carried the couple to the house and attempted to revive them. They poured cold water across their bodies and started massaging their limbs. Little by little, color came back into their faces. After two hours, Lydia began to gain consciousness. An hour later, Ingraham opened his eyes, reportedly demanding, "What is all this? Where are we?" Unfortunately, the brave Roger Elliot wasn't so lucky. He never recovered, and the lovers, who have come to be known as the "Frozen Couple of Owl's Head," were never able to thank him.

The Tale of the Loyal Assistant

In 1930, keeper Augustus B. Hamor came to Owl's Head with his springer spaniel, Spot. The faithful dog served by Hamor's side, assisting with many of the keeper's duties. He learned to bite down on the rope of the fog bell as ships approached, giving them fair warning. Then, he would race along the edge of the rocks and bark a greeting to each vessel as it passed. Ship's captains often blew their whistle or rang their own bell to thank Spot for his care.

One night, during an intense snowstorm, the captain of the mail boat *Matinicus* had not reached home at his usual hour, and his wife had become concerned. She called Mr. Hamor at the lighthouse to see if his dog had heard the whistle of her husband's boat. Sensing her alarm, the keeper sent Spot out into the biting storm. After thirty minutes, Spot returned and settled himself by the fire. Hamor could tell by his demeanor that he'd heard nothing. Just then, the dog leapt up from the hearth and ran back to the door. He scratched madly to be let out. Hamor could only assume that Spot had heard the ship's whistle at last. Relieved, he opened the door and followed his faithful companion out into the snow.

Spot labored through snowdrifts in a mad dash for the fog bell, but he couldn't reach it. Then, as if sensing the boat's danger, he made his way down the rocky promontory and ran to the edge of the water, barking hysterically. The captain heard him barking just in time, and steered his carrier away from the treacherous rocks. The *Matinicus* then gave three long whistle blasts to signal its appreciation.

Years later, when Spot died, his beloved keeper buried him near the fog bell he'd so faithfully tended.

The Tale of the Owl's Head Phantom

Like many lighthouses along America's shores, the Owl's Head Light is thought to be haunted—whether by the ghost of Roger Elliot or someone else, no one seems to know for sure. But there have been a number of unexplainable occurrences over the years.

For example, after snowstorms, mysterious footprints have been found to line the walk that leads to the lighthouse. The prints clearly belong to a man, size ten and a half. Perhaps the ghost of Roger Elliott retraces his steps along the snow-covered road. Or maybe Augustus Hamor has been out to visit his long-dead assistant. On occasion, keepers have reported seeing the specter, which resembles a man, in the windows of the lighthouse.

Whoever he is, the spirit at Owl's Head likes to be of assistance. From time to time, he polishes brass or frugally turns down the heat—a practice that seems to rule out the ghost of frozen seaman Roger Elliott.

Owl's Head Lighthouse is in West Penobscot Bay at the entrance to Rockland Harbor. Take U.S. 1 from Rockland to Route 73 south. Take 73 two miles south and turn left. Drive another two and a half miles and turn left on Lighthouse Road, just past the Owl's Head Post Office. A short distance up Lighthouse Road is a dirt parking lot. Park and walk around the barrier to find an impressive view of the lighthouse.

The lighthouse is closed to the public, but the grounds are open from Memorial Day through Labor Day, from 9 AM to sunset. For further information, contact Owl's Head Light State Park on Lighthouse Road, Owl's Head, Maine 04854, 207-941-4014; Website: www.state.me.us/doc/prkslnds/prkslnds.htm or contact The Rockland-Thomaston Area Chamber of Commerce: P.O. Box 508, Rockland, Maine 04841-0508, 207-596-0376.

Bob & Sandra Shanklin

Pensacola Lighthouse
Pensacola, Florida

A Lighthouse Built for One

Pensacola Lighthouse
Pensacola, Florida

Florida's hot summers send everyone searching for air conditioning; however, at Pensacola Lighthouse there is no need for it. Even when the heat is stifling, the air in the lighthouse is downright bone chilling. It's as if a cold, invisible force moves through the tower, inching its way through the cracks and sidling up to visitors as they make their way up the winding steps.

Haunted by the sounds of laughter that rattle the walls and windows, the lighthouse is shrouded in mystery. Doors slam on their own. The unmistakable smell of pipe tobacco floats gently upstairs when no one is smoking. Footsteps have been heard ascending and descending the staircase, and a glowing, ghost-like form has been spotted in the top window.

In the early nineteenth century, Pensacola Bay was a significant port. Its deep waters made navigation easy for trade ships, but with more and more traffic, a navigational light was needed to guide mariners safely to port. The lightship *Aurora Borealis* provided that much-needed beacon from June 23, 1823, until 1825. However, as was the norm then, the light was weak and didn't always provide adequate protection during storms. Moreover, it was often dry-docked for maintenance and out of commission. Clearly, a more permanent light station was in order.

The Pensacola Lighthouse took only two months to build; negotiations and clearance took almost three years. In 1826, it was completed on a 40-foot hill west of the Spanish Fort San Carlos de Barrancas. It was the fourth lighthouse in Florida, and no one yet knew that it would necessitate a fifth.

Unfortunately, the light's construction was shoddy and its placement ill-planned. The tower was too short, and the many trees around it often obstructed its beam. In 1847, changes were made to the reflector lenses, but in reality, they were temporary fixes that did little to aid in navigation. Sailors still had difficulty detecting the light. After repeated complaints, a 160-foot tower was erected 1,600 feet west of the original. This time, construction crews took their time. The tower was lit in 1859.

Shortly after its completion, the new lighthouse was taken over by Confederate soldiers. Officers broke in and stole oil and other supplies. Eventually, the lighthouse itself was used as a lookout tower during the siege of Fort Pickens, a Union stronghold across the bay. With Confederate cannons placed nearby, the lighthouse suffered its share of retaliatory fire by the Union army, but it ultimately survived. Over the years, it would survive its share of natural disasters as well. On several occasions, the Pensacola Light was struck by lightning and, in 1875, the tower fell victim to the Charleston Earthquake. Unfortunately, keeper Jeremiah Ingraham proved less resilient than the tower he tended.

In August 1826, Ingraham moved into the lighthouse with his young wife, Michaela Penalber. Michaela had all the characteristics of a proper lighthouse keeper's wife. She helped with the cleaning and maintenance. She stood by her husband while he tended the light and showed the lighthouse a great deal of deference, as any good wife would. However, it could be argued that, when all was said and done, she had cared for the lighthouse a little too much.

Though some believe Ingraham simply became ill and died, others believe that his wife murdered him when they were alone in the tower. It's a tantalizing theory, especially considering the fact that, after her husband's death, Michaela took over as keeper.

While not all believe that murder was to blame for the keeper's death, more than a few visitors have experienced unusual phenomena that suggest the presence of a decidedly perturbed spirit. The ghost in the Pensacola Lighthouse has been known to hurl objects at overnight guests in the keeper's quarters. One workman even described having a water hose yanked from his grip.

Moreover, when the lighthouse was refurbished in later years, blood—or something uncannily like it—was discovered in more than one room. Once hidden by layers of tile, the original wood floors revealed dark red stains that no amount of scrubbing has ever been able to remove. For those who had always suspected Michaela Ingraham a murderer, this was evidence enough.

Perhaps Jeremiah Ingraham is still trying to wrestle his lighthouse from the grasp of another. Or perhaps Michaela's jealous spirit is once again demanding exclusive ownership of her beloved dwelling. Whatever the case may be, the unsettling tale of Jeremiah and Michaela Ingraham is destined to leave its mark on the storied history of the Pensacola Light.

The Pensacola Lighthouse is located on the base of the Pensacola Naval Air Station, across the highway from the NAS museum. Take State 295 (Navy Boulevard) south out of Pensacola. The guards at the Naval Air Station can provide a car pass and directions to the lighthouse. Visitors may tour the grounds, but tours of the tower and keeper's quarters are restricted.

Lighthouse tours are given Sundays from noon to 4:00 PM, May through October. Tour the display center, which used to be the old keeper's quarters, and climb the 178 stairs to the top of the tower for a scenic view of Pensacola Bay. Historic exhibits are also available. Group tours are offered through the Coast Guard Office at 850-455-2354. For further information, contact the Pensacola Convention and Visitors Information Center: 1401 East Gregory Street, Pensacola, Florida 32501, 800-874-1234 or 850-434-1234; or contact the Pensacola Historical Society: 405 Adams Street, Pensacola, Florida 32501, 850-434-5455.

Fairport Harbor Light
Fairport Harbor, Ohio

The Light That Doesn't Look Haunted

Fairport Harbor Light
Fairport Harbor, Ohio

The Fairport Harbor Light isn't like most haunted places. Its furnishings are not covered in dust. The stairwells don't creak with age. Cold drafts don't shift through the room. The corridors don't howl when the wind slips through window cracks. No, the Fairport Harbor Light has been sufficiently restored. It was the lighthouse of the past, in its dilapidated state that looked haunted. At one time, razing it seemed the best thing to do. However, the people of Fairport realized how much they valued the old lighthouse. It had become a beacon of safety, a symbol of the past, and a historical marker. The citizens of Fairport Harbor banded together and asked that the government turn the lighthouse over to them for five years. The government agreed, on condition that the town raise funds for the building's restoration as well as find a use for it. Otherwise, they warned, the structure would be demolished.

The Fairport Harbor Historical Society succeeded in raising sufficient funds to refurbish the lighthouse, and in 1946, opened its doors to the public. The restored site became the first marine museum in Ohio and the first lighthouse museum on the Great Lakes. Today, about fifty volunteers maintain the lighthouse and run the museum.

In the early nineteenth century, before Fairport Harbor (then called Grandon) had developed as a port town, traffic began to increase in the harbor. Shortly, the need for a lighthouse arose. Several contractors bid on the project, but the contract was ultimately awarded to Jonathan Goldsmith and Hiram Wood and their bid of $2,900. They completed the tower and the keeper's house in 1825, but a dispute erupted over a cellar that was to be built beneath the keeper's dwelling. Goldsmith claimed that the cellar had never been a part of the bargain. He agreed to build the addition for an extra $174.30. The Collector of Customs in Cleveland, who was overseeing the project, had no choice but to accept this sum. Hiring a new contractor would prove even more costly.

The lighthouse was finally finished and activated by the fall of that same year. Ten years later, however, the foundation beneath Goldsmith's expensive lighthouse had settled so much so that a hefty sum of money was needed to restore what had only recently been built. Again, the Collector of Customs was forced to come up with a sum of money that had not been accounted for in the original budget. Ironically, six years later, Jonathan Goldsmith applied for the position of lighthouse keeper. Not surprisingly, the Collector of Customs flatly refused him. He wanted nothing whatsoever to do with man.

Problems with the Goldsmith-designed tower continued to trouble Fairport Harbor until the winter of 1869. By then, it had fallen into such ill repair that a temporary tower had to be erected so that the original could be torn down. The new contractors were given a budget of $30,000 to work with. However, after the foundation and twenty-nine courses had been laid, they experienced a setback. Funds were suspended, and work was delayed indefinitely, leaving the unfinished tower exposed to the elements. By the time construction resumed, another $10,000 was needed to repair damage done by the weather.

On August 11, 1871, the light was finally activated, and the harbor was officially rid of Jonathan Goldsmith's legacy. Captain Joseph Babcock was the next to the last of seventeen keepers in Fairport Harbor. He served the newer light from 1871 to 1919; thus, for a total of 48 years. He and his family worked together to man the lighthouse. In fact, one of his sons, Daniel, served as his assistant from 1901 to 1919 and eventually took over the duties of chief lighthouse keeper from 1919 to 1925. Sadly, another son, Robbie, never had the opportunity.

Young Robbie, who had been born in the lighthouse, died of smallpox at age five. Today, some believe that his ghost haunts the downstairs rooms. Staff members note cold air and a foul odor. They've also described feeling a pervasive sense of dread in this area of the lighthouse. They've experienced altogether different phenomena in other areas.

Evidence suggests that Robbie's is not the only spirit to haunt the Fairport Harbor Light. While in the lighthouse, Mrs. Babcock also became extremely ill and was ordered to remain in bed until she recovered. Confined to her bedroom, her only source of entertainment was a litter of several small kittens that played about her bedside and kept her company.

Mrs. Babcock favored one of the kittens in particular, the gray one. From her bed, she tossed a ball to it, and the kitten fetched it for her. The playful pet enlivened many a long afternoon for Mrs. Babcock in her upper-level room, and apparently, its game continues. Museum keepers and curators claim to see the ghost of the gray kitten scurrying about the floor, as if in pursuit of something.

Of course, as with any ghost story, there are skeptics. But recently, they were dealt a blow when workers installing air conditioning vents came upon the remains of a gray cat in the crawl space. Its mummified body is said to be kept in the lighthouse museum.

Much about the Fairport Harbor Lighthouse has changed over the years. Above all, it's gone from looking haunted to looking picturesque. But don't be fooled. There are some things that even renovations and a few coats of paint can't change.

Take Route 2 to the Fairport Harbor/ Richmond Street exit. Go north to the light at the Richmond Street/Route 283 intersection. Continue north approximately one-fourth mile to High Street. Follow High Street to the Fairport Harbor Lakefront Park entrance.

The Fairport Marine Museum, located in the downstairs of the old keeper's house, overlooks Fairport Harbor Lakefront Park. The lighthouse and museum are open Memorial Day through Labor Day. Group tours are available by appointment. The tower is open for climbing and provides visitors with spectacular views of the lake. For additional information and hours of operation, contact the museum at 129 Second Street, Fairport Harbor, Ohio 44077, 440-354-4825.

John Murray

Yaquina Bay Lighthouse
Newport, Oregon

The Dark Tower

Yaquina Bay Lighthouse
Newport, Oregon

Few visitors to the town of Newport, Oregon miss the chance to visit the Yaquina Bay Lighthouse. Built in 1871, it is the oldest building in Newport and the second-oldest lighthouse in Oregon. It remained active only three short years before a more impressive tower was built three miles north. Charles H. Pierce, his wife Sarah, and seven of their nine children lived in the lighthouse during its activation. However, it wasn't until long after the tower's deactivation that anyone took up permanent residence.

The Yaquina Bay Lighthouse has been cloaked in mystery for more than a hundred years. Gloomy hallways and a creaking spiral staircase are all part of its lure. A strange light in the third-floor window, smears of blood at the bottom of the third-floor staircase, and the eerie sound of screams reverberating against the lighthouse walls keep locals and visitors curious about the tower's past, which, according to legend, is dark. There were several mysterious deaths in the lighthouse. However, one story in particular has survived since the turn of the nineteenth century, and it is still very much alive in the Newport community.

Muriel, the delicate, sweet-tempered daughter of a sea captain, came to the shores of Newport with her father in 1899. It was the captain's intention to go back to sea while she remained on the island with relatives. She spent her first days alone, walking along the beach and sketching in notebooks, but it was not long before the amicable girl made friends. Together, she and her new acquaintances delighted in exploring the island, searching for adventure, and hoping to stumble upon mystery.

One dark night, she and her friends set out to explore the abandoned Yaquina Bay Lighthouse. Once inside, they crept up the stairs to the top of the tower and looked out over the vast stretch of sea before them. They began opening closet doors and mysterious panels. One iron door opened to a cavernous hole that appeared bottomless. Peering into the dank, black pit, the teens began scaring one another, and their wild imaginations got the better of them. As the empty lighthouse howled with the sounds of wind and screeching seabirds, the startled teens decided it was time to go.

Once outside and a good distance from the tower, young Muriel realized that she had forgotten her handkerchief. She returned with an escort to retrieve it. Not wanting to go back in himself, the boy elected to wait outside and stand guard. Muriel steeled herself for the task of reentering the dark tower. She planned to dash in and dash out and then be on her way. However, it didn't prove so simple a task.

When Muriel was out of sight, the boy heard a shriek and a call for help. The others heard it too and came running back to the lighthouse. They went inside to check on Muriel and found nothing but a pool of blood and her small, white handkerchief crumpled on the floor and spotted with blood. They proceeded up the stairwell and noticed a trail of blood leading to the iron trapdoor. The door, which had opened freely only moments earlier, was now locked. As much as they tried, Muriel's friends were unable to open the door. Frantically, they left the lighthouse in search of help.

For hours, search crews poured over the grounds and investigated the site. They searched from top to bottom, but no one found another trace of Muriel. It was as though she had vanished into thin air.

Detractors say that this story was originally a fictitious account written by Lischen M. Miller for an 1899 issue of the *Pacific Monthly*. Others, however, have reported seeing the young girl in the lighthouse and believe she haunts the tower.

Reportedly, a homeless man went to the lighthouse one rainy winter night in hopes of finding shelter. He ducked out of the rain and knocked on the door. To his surprise, the door opened, and a young girl stood before him. The figure disappeared, but he remained in the lighthouse all night, sheltered from the rain.

Members of the Coast Guard have also reported strange occurrences. One night, a Coast Guardsman noticed what looked like a person carrying a lantern in one of the lighthouse windows; before he could look again, the image had disappeared and the light dimmed. Other Coast Guardsmen claim to have seen a mysterious light emanating from the third-floor window. Though the beacon atop the tower is electrified, there is no reasonable explanation for this light.

Today the lighthouse serves as a museum. On

some mornings, museum keepers have difficulty opening the door, only to find, when they succeed, that pieces of merchandise had been moved during the night. Muriel very well may be behind these unexplained happenings; then again, so may the phantom that spirited her away all those years ago. Whatever the case, teenagers in Newport are liable to think twice before setting out to explore the Yaquina Bay Light on dark, uneventful nights.

Yaquina Bay Lighthouse sits on a bluff at the mouth of the Yaquina River. The tower is located in Yaquina Bay State Park on Highway 101 at the north end of the bridge. Paved trails and a walkway allow easy access to the top of the hill where the lighthouse sits. For those who have difficulty managing the walk, there is a parking lot at the back of the lighthouse. The parking entrance can be accessed using SW Government and Ninth Streets. The entrance fee is by donation.

A video about the lighthouse is shown in the basement. Private tours are available. For additional information, contact Friends of Yaquina Bay: 846 SW Government Street, Newport, Oregon 97365, 541-265-5679.

Bonnie K. Harrington

Yaquina Head Lighthouse
Newport, Oregon

The Taller Tower

Yaquina Head Lighthouse
Newport, Oregon

Yaquina Head Lighthouse replaced the light at Yaquina Bay in 1873, after the U.S. Lighthouse Board decided that Newport needed a taller tower. They got their wish. At 162 feet, Yaquina Head is the tallest tower on the Oregon coast. It still shines today after more than 130 years.

Like Yaquina Bay, Yaquina Head has experienced its share of mysterious deaths. During construction of the tower, two supply ships met their doom on its shores. Another story that circulates in Newport concerns a father and daughter who were staying in a hotel, named the Monterrey, between the Yaquina Bay and Yaquina Head towers. One evening, the father, Tom Briggs, was returning to his hotel when he was caught in a flooded creek and swept out to sea. When his daughter heard the news, she shot and killed herself. Ever since, locals have claimed to see her ghost wandering the beach between the two lighthouses. She appears most often during intense storms along the coastline, searching for her lost father.

Yet another story involves an assistant keeper named Herbert Higgins who served from 1918 to

1929. The main keeper, a man named Smith, had plans to go to the mainland for a brief stint. He wished to spend time with his family and get a small reprieve from his lighthouse duties. Higgins, his faithful assistant, had agreed to man the light and attend to maintenance while Smith was away. Smith had full confidence that Higgins could handle the job.

Several days after Smith went inland, Higgins became very ill. Weak and in need of bed rest, he was in no shape to tend the light. He asked another assistant keeper, Frank Story, to take on the responsibility. Hardly the ideal replacement, Story was careless and spent the evening drinking. When the time came to tend the light, he was in no condition, and Higgins realized it was up to him after all. With great effort, Higgins climbed the long, spiral staircase to the top of the tower. But the exertion proved too much. He collapsed in the tower of the lighthouse before he could light the lantern.

In the meantime, Smith had noticed from the mainland that the light was out. Sensing something awry, he returned immediately. Upstairs, he found Story drunk and Higgins, his assistant keeper, dead. Smith blamed himself. The lighthouse was his responsibility. He never should have left Higgins alone.

Soon after Higgins was laid to rest, Smith began to hear the sound of heavy footsteps climbing the vacant staircase. Guilty of conscience, he became unnerved and feared that Higgins' ghost had returned for retaliation. From then on, he was never alone in the lighthouse without his trusted bulldog, but that didn't stop the footsteps. They continued to haunt him for the rest of his tenure.

Take Highway 101 north about three miles from Newport. Turn west on Lighthouse Drive and follow signs to the Yaquina Head Outstanding Natural Area. The Interpretive Store and the Interpretive Center are open year-round. Tours are available daily from 12 PM-4 PM, weather permitting. There is a $5 charge per vehicle. For additional information, contact the Bureau of Land Management, Monday through Friday, at 541-574-3100.

Bob & Sandra Shanklin

Old Hilton Head (Leamington) Lighthouse
Hilton Head, South Carolina

The Lady in Blue

Old Hilton Head (Leamington) Lighthouse
Hilton Head, South Carolina

Towering pines and sweeping oaks shade the charming island of Hilton Head, South Carolina, where according to legend, a beautiful phantom wanders aimlessly beneath the trees. On dark summer nights, islanders have caught glimpses of a woman in a blue gossamer gown stealing across moon-dappled lawns. For years, the "Lady in Blue" has been as regular a fixture as the seagulls that dive in the water for silvery fish. The legend started many years ago, after a lighthouse keeper died tragically during a storm.

The first lighthouse on Hilton Head Island was built in 1881. Standing at an impressive height of 136 feet, the old lighthouse served in various capacities for years. Its shimmering light cast its beacon across the tumultuous Atlantic, safely guiding ships through the shipping channels. During World War II, the military used the lighthouse as a temporary base of operations. Anti-aircraft guns and ammunition sheds were placed carefully around the grounds, and the tower was used as a lookout for enemy ships.

Today, the lighthouse stands on the Leamington Plantation, behind the tall pine trees of the Arthur

Hills Golf Course at Palmetto Dunes Resort. A gated resort, Palmetto Dunes is a vacation spot for wealthy travelers. Amid such surroundings, the old lighthouse has been largely forgotten. There are no tours, no plaques or historical signs to mark its existence, and no light that radiates from its tower. Golfers usually whir by in their carts without ever glimpsing the deserted lighthouse hidden away in the trees. Though the Old Hilton Head (Leamington) Lighthouse is in many ways dead, the legend of the Lady in Blue is very much alive.

In 1893, a formidable storm slammed into the coast. Just twelve years after the lighthouse had been built, lighthouse keeper Adam Fripp was faced with the most brutal and devastating night of his life. Winds tore into the lighthouse and lifted trees right out of the ground. Waves rose and crashed with tremendous force, and rain fell in heavy torrents.

Inside the lighthouse, Fripp and his twenty-one-year-old daughter, Caroline, fought to keep the lantern burning. They fueled the light and watched as the savage storm ripped across the island. Suddenly, with one fatal gust of wind, the windows of the lantern room shattered, sending shards of glass throughout the room. Fripp and his daughter threw their arms to their faces just as the wind extinguished the light and rain began pouring in through the broken windows.

Fripp felt a sharp, gripping pain in his chest. He made for the light, but the pain was excruciating. He fell to the floor. With labored breath, he instructed his young daughter to keep the lantern burning. Caroline worked all night and all day to fulfill her father's dying wish. Then, three weeks later, she died. Some say she died of exposure. Others say she died of a broken heart.

Since that ill-fated night, Caroline's ghost has wandered the island in search of her lost father. Dressed in a long, blue gown, she's seen most often on stormy nights at the top of the old lighthouse. During long bouts of wind and rain, she stands in the top window, guarding the waters as she did on the night her father died.

The Hilton Head (Leamington) Lighthouse is located on the exclusive Arthur Hills Golf Course at Palmetto Dunes Resort on Hilton Head Island. The community is gated and exclusive to residents and those visiting the resort. The lighthouse is privately owned and can be viewed by appointment only. For further information, contact Greenwood Development Corporation: P.O. Box 5268, Hilton Head Island, South Carolina 29938, 803-785-1106, or contact the Hilton Head Island Historical Society at 843-785-3967.

Point Vicente Lighthouse
Rancho Palos Verdes, California

The Light That Burned Too Bright

Point Vicente Lighthouse
Rancho Palos Verdes, California

The glittering Point Vicente Lighthouse sits at the southwestern tip of the Palos Verdes Peninsula, atop a steep, rocky cliff that towers over the Pacific Ocean. Built some seventy-six years ago, it was the product of long petitioning by seafarers.

With the opening of the Panama Canal, traffic increased along the treacherous coast of Southern California. The rocky shoals in the area sent many a sailor to his grave. Knowing there was no way around that disastrous stretch of coastline, mariners risked their lives until appropriate measures were taken to protect them. On March 1, 1926, the U.S. Lighthouse Service acknowledged the danger of the waters and lit a two-million-candlepower white light. The Spanish-style tower was one of the last lighthouses built in California, but it was also one of the biggest, most powerful beacons along the California coast. Perched atop a cliff, the 67-foot tower rose 197 feet above sea level. Its beacon could be seen twenty miles out to sea. Ironically, however, there would come a time when this light would be considered altogether too powerful.

The Palos Verdes Peninsula was defended during World War II by the gun emplacements of Fort MacArthur. In order to prevent the infiltration of enemy forces, the Coast Artillerymen replaced the powerful 1,000-watt light with a 25-watt bulb. They also kept blackout curtains on the lighthouse windows in case an enemy vessel was spotted. Conceivably, the light could have offered navigational aid to enemies of war.

After the war, the lighthouse's powerful beam was found dangerous in other respects as well. To protect motorists on the mainland, keepers painted the walls and windows that faced inland white. This kept the tower's blinding light from streaming across Palos Verdes Drive and causing accidents.

Shortly thereafter, locals began to see a female silhouette in the windows of the lighthouse. This coincidence has led naysayers to argue that the image is merely a reflection of light across the painted surface. Coincidence or no, ghost stories have thrived in the Rancho Palos Verdes community ever since.

According to local lore, the soft, pale blue light of a female ghost haunts the Point Vicente Lighthouse. She has been described by those who have seen her as a tall, peaceful-looking woman in a long, white, flowing gown. She is affectionately referred to as the "Lady of the Light."

Some keepers believed that she was the wife of a sailor lost in the rocky waters, and many still accept this explanation. Even today, locals believe that she stands watch, waiting for the return of her husband's long-lost ship. Others have conjured up equally imaginative stories to explain her appearance: that she is the restless spirit of a woman who fell from the edge of a cliff one foggy night, or the spirit of a heartbroken lover who hurled herself into the restless waters. Still, more practical explanations attribute her existence to a shadow cast by the tower's prism lens.

Whatever her origin, one thing is certain: the Lady of the Light continues to feed the imaginations of those who live along this coast, where the light burns too bright.

Located in Rancho Palos Verdes on Palos Verdes Drive, the Point Vicente Lighthouse is about a quarter of a mile south of the southern end of Hawthorne Boulevard. Point Vicente is on eight acres at 31501 Palos Verdes Drive West, Rancho Palos Verdes, California 90275-5369. Visitors are permitted to tour the tower and outbuildings on the second Saturday of every month. Group tours are available by appointment only. The lighthouse and outbuildings are otherwise closed to visitors. For further information, call 310-541-0334.

Bob & Sandra Shanklin

Wood Island Light
Biddeford Pool, Maine

There Are No Happy Endings

Wood Island Light
Biddeford Pool, Maine

The dark and choppy waters off Biddeford Pool, Maine were once ideal for fishing. An abundance of lobster, mackerel, and herring brought an influx of fishermen to the area. But turbulent waters and vicious storms were ever present.

Even with the lighthouse, constructed in 1808, Biddeford Pool has remained an unpredictable and dangerous area. Voracious storms have slammed ships into the rocks and killed everyone onboard. At times, the lighthouse keeper or the warning light could do nothing to save a ship blown off course by the area's notoriously tempestuous weather.

In the past, such weather has made trips inland impossible. If, for example, there was an emergency at the light, and someone needed to see a doctor, life and death depended entirely on the weather. This was the case in 1960, when Coast Guardsman Laurier Burnham was tending the light without an assistant. His two-year-old daughter, Tammy, became extremely ill. He knew he had to get her to the mainland, but with no one to take over the lighthouse, he was forced to call on the Coast Guardsmen at the Fletcher Neck Lifeboat Station. Shortly after his call, two Coast Guardsmen arrived and took the child into their boat.

The waters that day were turbulent, and before the men knew it, their small boat had capsized. One man was able to grab hold of the boat and stay afloat, but the other, Edward Syvinski, was swept out to sea with the baby in his arms.

The Coast Guard searched for an hour before giving up, agreeing both their friend and the keeper's daughter were lost at sea. Burnham wasn't prepared to give up that easily. Despite orders to remain in the lighthouse, he left the tower unmanned and climbed aboard his own boat to search for his missing daughter. Against all odds, he finally found the two castaways near one of the neighboring islands, wearied from exhaustion but still alive. Turning his daughter over to another Coast Guard vessel, Burnham returned to the light. Little did he know the ordeal wasn't over.

Unbelievably, the second boat had trouble as well, and the crew was forced to turn the sick child over to a local lobsterman named Preston Alley. It was he who finally delivered Tammy Burnham to the Biddeford Pool hospital. In 1993, Tammy's father, Edward Syvinski, and Preston Alley were recognized by the South Portland Coast Guard Station for their extraordinary heroism. Unfortunately, not all of the island's tales end so happily.

Locals believe the island is haunted by the ghost of a man who committed a brutal murder at the end of the nineteenth century. According to a local tale, a twenty-five-year-old drifter came to the island and built a small shack on its western side. Easily bored with the calm of island life, he frequently visited the mainland's local pubs, where he drank himself into a stupor. One afternoon, the deputy sheriff came upon the young man in the street. The youth had just returned from a trip inland, drunk and belligerent. He wandered aimlessly and carried a long rifle. The lawman asked him to release his grip on the gun, but the young man refused. Then, without provocation, he shot the deputy sheriff in the gut and fled.

In a daze, the young man stumbled into the lighthouse. There, the keeper, Thomas Orcutt, questioned him and discovered what he'd done. Dutifully, the young drifter had reported his actions. He'd killed a man in cold blood. Orcutt knew the deputy that the boy had killed, but he managed to remain calm. He insisted that the boy return to the mainland immediately and turn himself in to the police. The drifter agreed to do just that, but in truth, he had other things in mind. He left Orcutt, returned to his shack, and shot himself in the head.

Since the murder-suicide, islanders have felt an eerie presence. Window shades are raised and lowered, locked doors unlock themselves and swing open, and open doors swing shut. And, locals have reported hearing a medley of unexplainable sounds.

The lighthouse keepers claim that the ghost lives with them. Perhaps the restless spirit of the troubled young drifter finds solace in the dwelling of his only confidant, keeper Thomas Orcutt.

Wood Island Light is located at the mouth of the Saco River, near Biddeford Pool, Maine. The lighthouse is listed on the National Historic Register and still serves as an active navigational aid. Accessible only by boat, Wood Island now serves as a wildlife sanctuary. The lighthouse is visible from the Biddeford Pool Trail, which is an Audubon Society trail on the mainland. A dock and boardwalk are open to visitors, however the tower is not. The lighthouse is managed by the Wood Island Lighthouse Society.

For additional information, contact Maine Audubon: 20 Gilsland Farm Road, Falmouth, Maine 04105, 207-781-2330; fax: 207-781-0974; email: info@maineaudubon.org

Bibliography

Books

Crompton, Samuel Willard. *The Lighthouse Book.* New York: Barnes and Noble Books, 1999.

Grant, John, and Ray Jones. *Legendary Lighthouses.* Old Saybrook: Globe Pequot Press, 1998.

Jones, Ray, and Bruce Roberts. *Northern Lighthouses: New Brunswick to the Jersey Shore.* Chester: The Globe Pequot Press, 1990.

Jones, Ray, and Bruce Roberts. *Southern Lighthouses: Chesapeake Bay to the Gulf of Mexico.* Chester: The Globe Pequot Press, 1989.

Schmidt-Lanigan, Therese. *Ghostly Beacons: Haunted Lighthouses of North America.* Atlglen: Whitford Press, 2000.

Snow, Edward Rowe. *The Lighthouses of New England.* New York: Dodd, Mead & Company, 1973.

Thomson, William O. *Lighthouse Legends & Hauntings.* Kennebunk: Scapes Me, 1998.

Online Sources

"Alcatraz Lighthouse." About.com. Updated 2002. Retrieved 9 Mar. 2002 http://gocalifornia. about.com/library/weekly/bl_lh_alc.htm

"Alcatraz Light: San Francisco, CA." Rudy and Alice Lighthouse Page. Updated Nov 2001. Retrieved 9 Mar. 2002 http://www.rudyalicelighthouse.net/CallLts/Alcatraz/ Alcatraz.htm

Bansemer, Roger. "Georgetown Lighthouse: North Island,
    S.C." RL Bansemer Homepage. Retrieved 5 Mar. 2002
    http://www.bansemer.com/nc-lighthouses
    /Georgetown_lighthouse.htm

Bansemer, Roger. "Ocracoke Light: Ocracoke Island, N.C." RL
    Bansemer Homepage. Retrieved 6 Mar. 2002
    http://www.bansemer.com/nc-lighthouses
    /Ocracoke_lighthouse.htm

Bansemer, Roger. "St. Simons Lighthouse: St. Simons Island,
    GA." RL Bansemer Homepage. Retrieved 4 Apr. 2002
    http://www.bansemer.com/Georgia_lighthouses/
    st_simons_lighthouse.htm.

"A Brief History of Alcatraz." National Park Service. Updated
    Nov. 2001. Retrieved 12 Mar. 2002
    http://www.bop.gov/ipapg/ipaalcatraz.html

D'Entremont, Jeremy. "Owl's Head Light." Coastlore
    Productions. Retrieved 26 Feb. 2002
    http://www.lighthouse.cc/owls/history.html

D'Entremont, Jeremy. "Wood Island Light: Biddeford Pool,
    Maine." Coastlore Productions. Updated Mar. 2002.
    Retrieved 4 Apr. 2002
    http://www.lighthouse.cc/ woodisland/history.html

DeWire, Elinor. "Dogs of the Lighthouses." *Dog Fancy.* 1997.
    Retrieved 2 Feb. 2002
    http://www.sentinelpublications.com/dogs.htm

Gamer, Thomas M. "Pensacola Lighthouse: Standing Guard
    for 173 Years." *The Pensacola Lighthouse.*
    Retrieved 4 Apr. 2002
    http://www.cyberpensacola.com/Cgaux/lighthouse.htm

"Ghost Hunt on Alcatraz Island." Southwest Ghost Hunter's
    Association. Updated Jan. 2002. Retrieved 9 Mar. 2002
    http://www.sgha.net/alcatraz.html

"Ghost Stories, Legends and Haunted Houses Come Alive in the Pensacola Area." Pensacola Visitor Information Center Official Site. Retrieved 19 Feb. 2002 http://www.visitpensacola.com/preskit/ haunted.asp

"Great Stories: Lighthouses of the South Atlantic." PBS Legendary Lighthouses. Public Broadcasting Station. Retrieved 12 Jan. 2002 http://www.pbs.org/ legendarylighthouses/html/satl.html

"The Haunted Doghouse." Dorpexpress. Retrieved 9 Mar. 2002 http://www.haunteddoghouse.com/alcatrezx.html

Hurley. Neil. "Pensacola Lighthouse History." Historic Lighthouse Publishers. Updated Nov. 1999. Retrieved 4 Apr. 2002 http://users.erols.com/lthouse/phs.htm

"The Legend of Blackboard." UNC School of Journalism and Mass Communication. Updated 1998. Retrieved 6 Mar. 2002 http://www.ibiblio.org/ghosts/bb2.html

"New London Ledge Light: New London, Connecticut." Coastlore Productions. Updated July 2001. Retrieved 4 Apr. 2002 http://www.lighthouse.cc/newlondonledge/ history.html

Pugh, Karl. "Blackboard's Ghost off the Coast of Ocracoke." The Free Lance-Star: Fredericksburg.com. 28 July 2001. Retrieved 6 March 2002 http://www.fredericksburg.com/News/FLS/2001/ 072001/07282001/347128

"The Rigid Silence: A Brief History ofAlcatraz Island." Ocean View Publishing. Updated 2000. Retrieved 12 Mar. 2002 http://www.alcatrazhistory.com/Rs1.htm

Shelton-Roberts, Cheryl. "[North Carolina's Lighthouses: Ocracoke Light] Lighthouse Society Notes." Updated 2002. Retrieved 11 Feb. 2002 http://www.outer-banks.com/lights/nocracoke.asp

"Tales from the Coast: Annie of the Lighthouse." Coastal Guide ICW-Net. Retrieved 5 Mar. 2002 http://www.icw-net.com/tales/gtannie.htm

Totton, Rick. "New London Ledge Light." Rick's Lighthouses. Updated 2000. Retrieved 4 Apr. 2002 http://www.rickslighthouses.com/ new_london_ledge.htm

Wlodarski, Rob, and Anne Wlodarski. "America's Most Haunted Places: Haunted Alcatraz." Prairie Ghosts. Updated 2001. Retrieved 9 Mar. 2002 http://www.prairieghosts.com/gpalcatraz.html

Video

Steitz, George C. (Dir.). *Haunted Lighthouses*. Impact Television Productions, 1999.